Love Not the World

Love Not the World

by
John MacArthur, Jr.

MOODY PRESS
CHICAGO

© 1986 by
JOHN F. MACARTHUR, JR.

All Scripture quotations, unless noted otherwise, are from the *New Scofield Reference Bible*, King James Version. Copyright © 1967 by Oxford University Press, Inc. Reprinted by permission.

The use of selected references from various versions of the Bible in this publication does not necessarily imply publisher endorsement of the versions in their entirety.

ISBN: 0-8024-5098-9

3 4 5 6 7 Printing/EP/Year 91 90 89

Printed in the United States of America

Contents

These Bible studies are taken from messages delivered by Pastor-Teacher John MacArthur, Jr., at Grace Community Church in Panorama City, California. The recorded messages themselves may be purchased as a series or individually. Please request the current price list by writing to:

WORD OF GRACE COMMUNICATIONS
P.O. Box 4000
Panorama City, CA 91412

Or call the following toll-free number:
1-800-55-GRACE

1

How Do You Know You're a Christian?

Outline

Introduction
A. The Definition
B. The Difficulties
   1. The appearance of salvation
   2. The assurance of salvation
     a) Objective assurance
     b) Subjective assurance
       (1) 2 Corinthians 1:12
       (2) 1 John 5:10
       (3) Romans 8:14-16

Lesson
I. The Principle (vv. 3-5)
  A. The Premise of Obedience (v. 3)
    1. The assurance of knowing
    2. The analysis of keeping
     a) The explanation of keeping
     b) The extent of keeping
     c) The examples of keeping
       (1) John 14
       (2) John 15
       (3) Psalm 116
  B. The Pretense of Faith (v. 4)
    1. Explained
    2. Expressed
     a) Titus 1:16
     b) Luke 6:46
     c) Matthew 7:22-23
    3. Exposed
  C. The Perfection in Love (v. 5)
    1. Stated
    2. Illustrated

II. The Pattern (v. 6)
   A. Identified
   B. Illustrated
      1. In the humility of Christ
         a) The precept
         b) The pattern
      2. In the submission of Christ
         a) John 6:38
         b) John 8:29
         c) John 10:18
         d) John 14:31
III. The Precept (vv. 7-11)
   A. The Commandment (vv. 7-8)
      1. An old message (v. 7)
      2. A new meaning (v. 8)
   B. The Contrast (vv. 9-11)

Introduction

A. The Definition

First John 2:3-11 tells us how we can know we are Christians. If we were to conduct a man-on-the-street interview, asking people what it means to be a Christian, we would probably receive several different answers. There are many opinions of what a Christian is. The basic definition is one who believes in the Lord Jesus Christ as Savior and Lord. The one who does not believe is not a Christian. Jesus stated that definition very simply when He said, "He that believeth on him is not condemned; but he that believeth not is condemned already, because he hath not believed in the name of the only begotten Son of God" (John 3:18).

B. The Difficulties

   1. The appearance of salvation

   The issue of determining who is a Christian becomes difficult when considering people who claim to believe. Many who profess to believe in Christ may act like Christians to a certain degree, but they turn out to be impostors or are simply misinformed about the nature of salvation. Either way, it becomes obvious that they did not really know the truth. For example, 1 John 2:19 identifies some people who claimed to be Christians but eventually left the fellowship: "They were not of us; for if they had been of us, they would no doubt have continued with us; but they went out, that they might be made manifest that they were not all of us." One way you can identify false Christians (who are called "tares" in Matt. 13:38) is that they will abandon Christianity. But while they're interacting with true believers, it is difficult to tell them apart.

2. The assurance of salvation

A further difficulty comes in the lives of people who wonder if they are saved. Many of them have doubts and need evidence. Unfortunately, some of them who aren't Christians have wrongly been told that their superficial beliefs are sufficient to save them, so they assume that they're Christians when they really aren't. In 2 Peter 1:9-10 Peter explains how a believer can be assured of his salvation: "He that lacketh [the qualities of spiritual maturity] is blind and cannot see afar off, and hath forgotten that he was purged from his old sins. Wherefore the rather, brethren, give diligence to make your calling and election sure; for if ye do these things, ye shall never fall." Peter was not talking about the loss of salvation but the assurance of salvation. There are certain Christians who can't remember that they have been saved. They lack the confidence of knowing they're saved because they lack faith, virtue, knowledge, self-control, patience, godliness, brotherly kindness, and love (vv. 5-7). The manifestation of godly works in our lives assures us that something has transformed us. If we don't see those things, we may question whether any change took place. Therefore, Peter encourages us to make sure those qualities are in our lives so we can have the security of knowing we're saved.

How do you know you're really a Christian? That is a crucial question. The Scriptures give several elements of assurance that can show us if we're truly saved. They can be categorized under the topics of objective assurance and subjective assurance.

a) Objective assurance

Objective assurance comes from outside us; it is based on the godly things the Spirit produces in our lives. That's what Peter is talking about in 2 Peter 1. If you see those things in your life, it will confirm in your mind that you're truly saved.

3

b) Subjective assurance

Subjective assurance is based on something within us, namely, the witness of the Spirit. Whereas the former type of assurance is visible, the latter is invisible. Our internal assurance is described in several passages in the New Testament.

(1) 2 Corinthians 1:12—Paul said, "Our rejoicing is this, the testimony of our conscience, that in simplicity and godly sincerity, not with fleshly wisdom but by the grace of God, we have behaved ourselves in the world." Paul was saying, "I know what's going on in my life because of the testimony of my conscience. Something rings true in my conscience that my behavior is pleasing to God."

(2) 1 John 5:10—"He that believeth on the Son of God hath the witness in himself." That indwelling witness who bears testimony to Christ is the Holy Spirit. He attests to the validity of a believer's salvation.

(3) Romans 8:14-16—"As many as are led by the Spirit of God, they are the sons of God. For ye have not received the spirit of bondage [legalism] again to fear; but ye have received the Spirit of adoption, whereby we cry, Abba, Father" (vv. 14-15). "Abba" is the equivalent to *daddy*, an endearing term. It implies that we can relate to God as a child talks to his loving father. Verse 16 tells us that the indwelling Spirit gives us the confidence to enter God's presence: "The Spirit himself beareth witness with our spirit, that we are the children of God." The internal witness of the Spirit in our lives is of little help to others because no one can read our hearts. But that kind of confirmation is helpful to us.

The apostle John deals with objective assurance in 1 John 2. The visible proof to the individual, the church, and the world that you are a Christian is the attitudes and actions that are produced by the Holy Spirit in your life. When anyone tells me they have doubts about their Christianity, the first questions I usually ask are: Have you applied yourself to godliness? Are you reading the Word? Are you spending time in prayer? Are you learning the Word

4

of God? Are you desiring to draw near to God and to obediently follow the Holy Spirit? If you can answer yes to those questions, you will have confirmation that you're a believer because the fruits of salvation are visible in your life. That is the theme of 1 John 2:3-11. The apostle John provides two tests by which we can evaluate the claims of a person who professes to be a Christian.

Two Tests That Tell the Truth

1. The doctrinal test

   a) Do you confess Christ?

   A person's beliefs about Christ will validate his claim to be a Christian. The Greek word translated "confess" means "to say the same thing." The first part of the doctrinal test asks about the person in question. Does he say the same thing about Christ that God says in the Bible? If he says, "I'm a Christian, but I don't believe Christ is God," then he's not saying the same thing about Christ that God says. He is not confessing Christ.

   (1) 1 John 2:22-23—"Who is a liar but he that denieth that Jesus is the Christ? He is antichrist, that denieth the Father and the Son. Whosoever denieth the Son, the same hath not the Father; He that confesseth the Son hath the Father also."

   (2) 1 John 4:2—"By this know ye the Spirit of God: every spirit that confesseth that Jesus Christ is come in the flesh is of God."

   (3) 1 John 5:1—"Whosoever believeth that Jesus is the Christ is born of God."

   Being truly saved is a matter of confessing, or agreeing, that Jesus is the Christ.

   b) Do you confess your sin?

   A Christian says the same thing about his sin that God says. If someone comes along and tells me he's a Christian but doesn't acknowledge his sin, I don't believe him.

   (1) 1 John 1:6, 8—"If we say that we have fellowship with him, and walk in darkness, we lie. . . . If we say that we have no sin, we deceive ourselves, and the truth is not in us."

5

(2) 1 John 1:9-10—Verse 9 tells us that if we are confessing sin, then we are the ones being forgiven—we are the true Christians. Verse 10 says, "If we say that we have not sinned, we make him a liar, and his word is not in us."

2. The moral test

   a) Do you obey God's Word?

   First John 2:3 says, "By this we do know that we know him, if we keep his commandments."

   b) Do you love others?

   First John 2:10 says, "He that loveth his brother abideth in the light."

The issue in 1 John 2:3-11 is the objective moral test of true Christianity: obedience and love. The Christians John wrote to were being influenced by false teachers, or "antichrists," according to 1 John 2:18. Therefore, John exhorts his readers to "test the spirits" (4:1) rather than to naively believe their claims. If they could see obedience and love in the lives of the teachers, those qualities would attest to their spiritual lives.

Lesson

I. THE PRINCIPLE (vv. 3-5)

   A. The Premise of Obedience (v. 3)

   "And by this we do know that we know him, if we keep his commandments."

   1. The assurance of knowing

   In chapter 1, the phrases "walk in the light" and "have fellowship one with another" (v. 7) are synonymous with the phrase "know him" in verse 3 of chapter 2. The Greek verb translated "know" is *ginōskō*. Emphasizing its present and perfect-tense forms, the verse could be translated, "By this are we continually knowing that we have already come to know Him." Although a Christian has already come to know Christ, he needs to have confidence that his knowledge of Christ has resulted in salvation. John says we can know Christ has saved us "if we keep his [Christ's] commandments." Obedience is one way of knowing you're a Christian. If a person claims to be a Christian but is disobedient to God throughout his life, the apostle John says he's "a liar, and the truth is not

6

in him" (v. 4). The way to be assured that we truly know Him as a child knows his father is by keeping His commandments. Obedience results in assurance. Christians who have doubts usually are involved in sin, because sin breeds doubt.

2. The analysis of keeping

   a) The explanation of keeping

   The Greek word translated "keep" conveys the idea of a watchful, observant obedience. It is not an obedience that is the result of external pressure, which might cause someone to say, "I have to do this, because I'm afraid that if I don't I'll get whacked by the divine hammer!" The term is more than just the act of obeying the commands. It is a holy desire to obey God because you love Him. Rather than being a negative fear, obedience is inspired by love to become your heart's greatest desire. You are to keep Christ's commands in the spirit of obedience. Henry Alford's *Greek Testament* defines "keep" as "guarding, as some precious thing" (vol. 4 [Chicago: Moody, 1968], p. 434). The Christian can know that he knows God when the great desire of his heart is to obey Him. The present tense implies that we are to continually keep His commandments. The habitual moment-by-moment safeguarding of our obedience to the Word of God is a sign of our salvation. When people claim to be Christians and then live any way they please, in complete disregard of God's command, they undermine their claim.

   For "commandments" the apostle did not use the Greek word *nomos*, which refers to the law of Moses, but the word *entolē*, which refers to the precepts of Christ. We are to keep the precepts of Christ, who is the antecedent of the pronoun "his" in verse 3. We can identify a Christian because he keeps the precepts of Christ, not because he subscribes to the law of Moses. John did not say, "By this do we know that we know him, if we keep the law of Moses." But if we desire to obey and honor the precepts of Christ, we prove that we have come to a saving knowledge of God and the Lord Jesus Christ. When a person becomes a Christian, he acknowledges Jesus Christ as

7

Lord. If His authority is gladly received, then obedience is a foregone conclusion.

b) The extent of keeping

Who can continue to keep the commandments? Since it is the ones who continue to keep His commandments who know God (v. 3), and Christians are the ones who know God (v. 13), then it follows that Christians are the only ones who can keep His commandments. The New Testament says that the unregenerate are the "children of disobedience" (Eph. 2:2, KJV*). You don't need a lecture on human nature to understand that people are disobedient. Just look at your kids—we all enter life that way. Conversely, 1 Peter 1:14 identifies the regenerate as "obedient children." If you're not obedient, then you're not a Christian.

c) The examples of keeping

If you try to be obedient, you may wonder if you obey enough. Can a Christian's life ever be characterized by absolute obedience? You must understand the distinction between legal obedience and gracious obedience. Gracious obedience pertains to God's desire for us to exhibit a loving and sincere spirit of obedience. Although it is marked by defects, it is still accepted by God, and its blemishes are blotted out by the blood of Jesus Christ. The obedience that our Lord is after is not legal obedience qualified by law but gracious obedience qualified by love. It's not based on fear; it's based on friendship.

(1) John 14—Before He ascended into heaven, Jesus might have said, "Now, men, I'm leaving. One false move in My absence and you're going to get it!" If He had, they might have spent the rest of their lives in spiritual apoplexy. What He actually said was, "If ye love me, keep my commandments" (v. 15). Obeying the Lord is not connected with law or fear; it is connected with love. Verses 21 and 23 say, "He that hath my commandments, and keepeth them, he it is that loveth me. . . . If a man love me, he will keep my words."

*King James Version.

8

(2) John 15—"If ye keep my commandments, ye shall abide in my love, even as I have kept my Father's commandments, and abide in his love. . . . Greater love hath no man than this, that a man lay down his life for his friends. Ye are my friends, if ye do whatever I command you" (vv. 10, 13-14).

(3) Psalm 116—The psalmist expressed the spirit of obedience when he said, "What shall I render unto the Lord for all his benefits toward me?" (v. 12). God is not expecting absolute perfection. As a Christian, you don't need to live under the fear that if you ever do something wrong, you're going to be severely punished and lose your salvation. God is looking for a spirit of obedience. True Christians have a desire to submit to Jesus Christ even though they can't always make that desire come to pass. God understands that.

B. The Pretense of Faith (v. 4)

"He that saith, I know him [Christ], and keepeth not his commandments, is a liar, and the truth is not in him."

1. Explained

The word "truth" refers to Christ. The person who doesn't obey Christ's commands doesn't have Christ or His truth in his heart. John's point here is that Christians obey; non-Christians do not. Nonbelievers do not submit to the lordship of Christ; they fulfill their own desires at their own pace. John says they may claim to know Him, but if they do not keep His commandments, they are liars.

2. Expressed

a) Titus 1:16—"They profess that they know God, but in works they deny him, being abominable, and disobedient." False believers fail the moral test. They make a profession of faith, but their lives don't support it. Disobedience refutes the validity of such claims.

b) Luke 6:46—Jesus said to the multitudes, "Why call ye me, Lord, Lord, and do not the things which I say?"

c) Matthew 7:22-23—There are going to be many people at the great white throne judgment (Rev. 20:11-15) who will say, "Lord, Lord, have we not prophesied in thy name? And in thy name have cast out demons? And in thy name done many wonderful works? And then will [Jesus] profess unto them, I never knew you; depart from me."

3. Exposed

Any claim to know Christ that is not accompanied by a spirit of gracious obedience is a lie. John exposes the vain pretenses of Gnostics or anyone else who makes this claim. He also gives a fatal blow to antinomianism, which is an extreme abuse of grace that sets all commandments aside because Christ already paid the penalty of sin. But John says a true Christian desires to obey Christ. Many claim to know God, but I doubt all really do. I'm reminded of a nightclub owner who said, "I wouldn't be where I am today if it weren't for the Big Man upstairs." All kinds of people claim to know God—but proving it is something else.

C. The Perfection in Love (v. 5)

"But whosoever keepeth his word, in him verily is the love of God perfected; by this know we that we are in him."

The word "whosoever" is important because it refutes the Gnostic heresy that claimed spiritual union with God was just for the elite. It doesn't restrict the ability to keep the Word to a select few. The verb "keepeth" implies a continual guarding of the Word. Whoever's life is characterized by a spirit of gracious obedience has the love of God perfected in him. "The love of God," if understood to be an objective genitive in the Greek text, refers to our love for God, which is perfected in obedience. We make our love for God obvious by keeping His commandments.

1. Stated

Our love for God is made visible by our obedience. True love for God is not sentiment or some mystical experience. It is moral obedience. John said this about our love for God and His love for us: "No man hath seen God at any time. If we love one another, God dwelleth in us, and his love is perfected in us. . . . And we have known and believed the love that God hath to us. God is love, and he that dwelleth in love dwelleth in God, and God in him" (1 John 4:12, 16). Love is made manifest in our obedience and is evidence that we are saved.

10

2. Illustrated

There was a man whose profession was religion. He was
a member of the Jewish Sanhedrin, and his name was
Saul, better known to us as Paul. He became very
indignant because there was a new heresy around by the
name of Christianity. Its central doctrine was that Jesus
Christ—apparently a criminal who had been crucified a
few years before—was alive. Paul approved the stoning
of Stephen, the first Christian martyr. From then on, he
decided to make it his business to imprison and kill
Christians, "breathing out threatenings and slaughter
against the disciples of the Lord" (Acts 9:1).

One day, while he was on his way to Damascus with
special papers from the religious leaders of Jerusalem
giving him the right to incarcerate and persecute Christians, God struck him flat on his face. Saul of Tarsus said,
"Who art Thou, Lord?" (Acts 9:5). He recognized that
whoever spoke was clearly superior to him. After Christ
revealed Himself to Saul, the humbled persecutor said,
"Lord, what wilt thou have me to do?" (v. 6). There is no
such thing as Christianity without obedience. The very
first thing Paul thought of when he submitted to the
lordship of Christ was what he should do. Later (Romans
7) he stated that in his heart he delighted in the law of
God (v. 22).

II. THE PATTERN (v. 6)

"He that saith he abideth in him ought himself also so to walk,
even as he walked."

The Bible often gives us a principle and then a pattern of someone
we can follow. The apostle Paul told the Corinthians to follow
him because he was following Christ (1 Cor. 11:1).

A. Identified

Whether John says "abiding in him," "knowing him," "walking in the light," or "being in the fellowship," he is referring
to salvation. If we say we are Christians, we ought to be
patterning ourselves after Christ. Verse 6 doesn't say we will
be exactly like Him, but it does say we ought to be. We owe
that much to Him. The word "abideth" is a Johannine term
used repeatedly in John 15, where the apostle tells us that the

11

true branch abides in the vine. In other words, true Christians remain in vital, living relationship to Christ. We ought to live like He lived. As a Christian who shares Christ's eternal life, we can live like Christ because the same Holy Spirit that empowered Him lives in us.

B. Illustrated

1. In the humility of Christ

   a) The precept

   Philippians 2:2 says, "Fulfill ye my joy, that ye be like-minded." Paul wanted the Philippians to quit arguing and have "the same love, being of one accord, of one mind" (v. 2). In verses 3-4 he tells them they can do that by being humble: "Let nothing be done through strife or vainglory, but in lowliness of mind let each esteem others better than themselves. Look not every man on his own things, but every man also on the things of others." Humility breeds love. Now he could have stopped there with the principle, but he went a step further to give his readers a pattern.

   b) The pattern

   Verses 5-8 say, "Let [the same] mind be in you, which was also in Christ Jesus, who, being in the form of God, thought it not robbery to be equal with God, but made himself of no reputation, and took upon him the form of a servant, and was made in the likeness of men; and, being found in fashion as a man, he humbled himself." Look at the pattern of Jesus. Never did anyone of such high position stoop to such a low position. Jesus is the greatest illustration of humility there ever was.

2. In the submission of Christ

   John says that if you claim to be a Christian, you ought to live as Jesus lived. The word "walk" refers to one's manner of life. Your manner of life ought to be Christlike. That requires obedience to God's standards. Did you know that Christ was obedient? He obeyed the Mosaic law to the very letter. He obeyed the divine stipulations of His messiahship. John's gospel emphasizes Christ's obedience to the Father's will.

12

a) John 6:38—Jesus said, "I came down from heaven, not to do mine own will but the will of him that sent me."

b) John 8:29—"He that sent me is with me. The Father hath not left me alone; for I do always those things that please him."

c) John 10:18—"No man taketh [my life] from me, but I lay it down of myself. I have power to lay it down, and I have power to take it again. This commandment have I received of my Father."

d) John 14:31—"That the world may know that I love the Father, and, as the Father gave me commandment, even so I do." Jesus' submissive obedience is the pattern we are to trace our lives upon. The kind of obedience that characterized Christ is to be true of us. Do you think it was burdensome for Jesus to obey the Father? Not at all!

III. THE PRECEPT (vv. 7-11)

John gives us a general principle of obedience and then the specific precept of loving others in verses 7 through 11. The primary issue of the moral test is obeying the command to love. You may wonder what's so important about loving. Jesus reveals its high priority in Matthew 22:37-40 when He says, "Thou shalt love the Lord, thy God, with all thy heart, and with all thy soul, and with all thy mind. This is the first and great commandment. And the second is like it, Thou shalt love thy neighbor as thyself. On these two commandments hang all the law and the prophets." If you keep the commandments of loving God and others, you don't have to worry about any of the rest. That is the essence of the Christian life. If you do that, then you can do what you want because you will have automatically fulfilled the law. Romans 13:8-10 says, "Owe no man any thing, but to love one another; for he that loveth another hath fulfilled the law. For this, Thou shalt not commit adultery, Thou shalt not kill, Thou shalt not steal, Thou shalt not bear false witness, Thou shalt not covet; and if there be any other commandment, it is briefly comprehended in this saying, namely, Thou shalt love thy neighbor as thyself. Love worketh no ill to its neighbor; therefore, love is the fulfilling of the law." If you love your neighbor as yourself, you don't need a command that says not to kill your neighbor or commit adultery with your neighbor's wife. Love precludes it.

A. The Commandment (vv. 7-8)

  1. An old message (v. 7)

"I write no new commandment unto you, but an old commandment which ye had from the beginning. The old commandment is the word which ye have heard from the beginning."

The last three words of the verse do not appear in the best Greek manuscripts. The word translated "new" is not *neos*, meaning "new in time," but *kainos*, meaning "new in quality." It refers to something that would replace what has been worn out. John is saying, "I'm not giving you something you've never heard of before. I'm just telling you an old commandment that you've heard from the beginning—from the first time you heard the gospel."

  2. A new meaning (v. 8)

"Again, a new commandment I write unto you, which thing is true in him and in you, because the darkness is past, and the true light now shineth."

Verse 7 sounds like a contradiction of verse 8. After stating that he is giving his readers an old commandment, John now says he is writing a new commandment. Since the commandments are similar, knowing what one is can help us identify the other. In John 13:34 Jesus says, "A new commandment I give unto you, that ye love one another." Loving one another is not a new commandment because the Old Testament instructs believers to do that. However, Jesus gave it new meaning by qualifying that love with the phrase "As I have loved you" (v. 34). It's one thing for God to say, "Love one another," but when God personally demonstrated that love by coming to earth as a man, it became a fresh commandment. The Old Testament commandment to love others received new meaning from Jesus.

There are two tests of a true Christian: the doctrinal test (Does he confess Christ and sin?) and the moral test (Does he have the spirit of gracious obedience, and does he love the brethren?). The new commandment that Jesus spoke of is part of the moral test. John said that the new commandment of loving others was seen in Christ and should also be evident in us. Romans 5:5 tells us that "the love of God is shed abroad in our hearts." Love is a new commandment only in the sense that Christ raised it

14

to a new standard in the church. Jesus showed us what love is and said we are to love as He did. Then He planted that love in us by His indwelling Spirit. If you say you are a Christian, I have two questions for you: Do you have a spirit of obedience toward Jesus Christ? Do you love your Christian brothers? Those are not suggestions but necessary qualities in the life of a true believer.

B. The Contrast (vv. 9-11)

"He that saith he is in the light, and hateth his brother, is in darkness even until now. He that loveth his brother abideth in the light, and there is no occasion of stumbling in him. But he that hateth his brother is in darkness, and walketh in darkness, and knoweth not where he goeth, because darkness hath blinded his eyes."

These verses attack the hypocrisy of the Gnostics, who claimed to be in the light but didn't love the Christian brethren. That revealed they were still in darkness. Your claim to be a Christian is valid only if it's verified by a life of love. The Gnostics believed that only the elite had the necessary knowledge for salvation, and they lorded their supposed superiority over others.

Verse 10 does not mean you're going to have affection for every Christian you meet. It just means that you have a spirit of love toward your Christian brothers. False Christians ("tares") won't exhibit that kind of love. In fact, tares can't put up with Christians very long—they eventually begin to resent true believers and despise everything they stand for. However, true Christians love the brotherhood. The Christian who loves knows where he's going. He walks in the light and doesn't stumble. That is evidenced by his obedience and his love. The one who does not love is in the darkness. If you habitually conduct yourself in a sphere of darkness that is void of love, you are not saved.

How do you know who is a Christian? The doctrinal test asks: Is he confessing Christ and sin? The moral test asks: Is his life characterized by obedience and love? Examine your heart to see if you are a true Christian or if you have been deceived into believing you are saved. Consider these penetrating words from Jesus: "Not every one that saith unto me, Lord, Lord, shall enter into the kingdom of heaven, but he that doeth the will of my Father, who is in heaven. Many will say to me in that day, Lord, Lord. . . . And then will I profess unto them, I never knew you; depart from me, ye that work iniquity" (Matt. 7:21-23).

Focusing on the Facts

1. What is the basic definition of a Christian (see p. 2)?
2. Why is it hard to identify who is a Christian? What is one way you can identify false Christians, according to 1 John 2:19 (see pp. 2-3)?
3. What does Peter exhort Christians to do so that they can be assured of their salvation (2 Pet. 1:5-10; see p. 3)?
4. Compare the objective and subjective types of assurance of salvation. What type of assurance does John deal with in 1 John 2 (see pp. 3-5)?
5. What is the visible proof that a person is a Christian (see p. 4)?
6. Identify the two parts of the doctrinal test of salvation and support each part with a verse from Scripture (see pp. 5-6).
7. Identify the two parts of the moral test and support each part with a verse from Scripture (see p. 6).
8. Why do Christians who are sinning have doubts about their salvation (see p. 7)?
9. Explain the type of obedience the word "keep" conveys (see p. 7).
10. Explain the difference between legal and gracious obedience (see p. 8).
11. What does the apostle John say about the person who does not obey the commands of Christ (1 John 2:4; see p. 9)?
12. What did the Gnostics claim about spiritual union with God? What one word refutes that in 1 John 2:5 (see p. 10)?
13. How should the true nature of our love for God be expressed? How should it not be expressed (see p. 10)?
14. What was Paul's response when Christ revealed Himself on the road to Damascus (Acts 9:6)? What is the significance of that (see p. 11)?
15. After first giving us a principle, what does the Bible often give us next (see p. 11)?
16. What do the phrases "abiding in him," "knowing him," "walking in the light," and "being in the fellowship" refer to (see p. 11)?
17. What enables the Christian to live like Christ (see p. 12)?
18. Identify the precept and the pattern that are given in Philippians 2:2-8 (see p. 12).
19. How did Christ show His submission to the Father? Support your answer with Scripture (see pp. 12-13).
20. How did Jesus give an old commandment new meaning (John 13:34; see pp. 14-15)?
21. Identify the hypocrisy noted in 1 John 2:9-11 (see p. 15).

Pondering the Principles

1. It is important to evaluate whether a person is saved. If someone is self-deceived into believing he is a Christian, you may be able to discern that and lead him to a true saving knowledge of Christ. If you need to select someone to serve on a decision-making committee at your church, you must choose a true believer, who can be led by the Spirit. Suppose you hear a guest speaker at church or hear a preacher on television. How will you discern the validity of what he is saying unless his claims and life verify that he is truly a servant of God? Paul warned the Ephesian church that it would be attacked by false teachers from within and without (Acts 20:28-30). John encouraged his readers to "test the spirits to see whether they are from God, because many false prophets have gone out into the world" (1 John 4:1, NIV*). Memorize the questions on pages 5-6 for both the doctrinal and the moral tests. Don't be naively misled by someone who claims to know the truth but really doesn't.

2. Do you love God? Do you love the children of God? These questions demand a soul-searching examination because it is easy to assume the answer is yes. Meditate on 1 John 3:14-18; 4:7-11, 19-21; and 5:1-3. What proof is there in your life that you love God and His children? When you read Scripture or are instructed by your pastor, do you act upon those truths? When you see needs that you are able to meet, do you seek to meet them? Commit yourself to expressing your love for God and others on a daily basis. In so doing, you will never lack assurance of your salvation (1 John 3:14; 5:2).

*New International Version.

2
The Love God Hates—
Part 1

Outline

Introduction
A. The Antithesis in God's Character
   1. God's love
   2. God's hatred
      a) Psalm 97:10
      b) Psalm 119
B. The Analysis of the Epistle's Context
   1. The thematic context
      a) Surveyed
      b) Specified
      c) Supported
   2. The historical context
      a) Examined
      b) Exemplified
C. The Application to Modern Christians

Lesson
I. Because of What the World Is (v. 15)
A. The Definition of the World
   1. The earth
   2. The human race
   3. The evil system
B. The Description of the World
   1. Its prince
   2. Its people

Conclusion

Introduction

A. The Antithesis in God's Character

   1. God's love

      The Bible is clear that God is a God of love. I doubt that anyone familiar with Christianity would argue that point. The apostle John emphasizes God's love in his epistle. For example, in 1 John 4:7-8 we read, "Beloved, let us love one another; for love is of God, and everyone that loveth is born of God, and knoweth God. He that loveth not knoweth not God; for God is love." Verse 11 says, "Beloved, if God so loved us, we ought also to love one another." And verse 16 says, "We have known and believed the love that God hath to us. God is love, and he that dwelleth in love dwelleth in God, and God in him."

   2. God's hatred

      Because God loves, He also hates. There can be no love unless there is the antithesis of love, which is hate. Those two emotions are inseparable. For example, if you love someone, you hate whatever it is that would harm that person. If you're a parent, you hate anything that would harm your children. If you're married, you hate anything that would defile or injure your spouse. If you love good, then you hate evil. If you love God, you hate Satan. If you love unity, you hate discord.

      Some scriptural examples of the relationship between love and hate are found in the psalms.

      a) Psalm 97:10—"Ye who love the Lord, hate evil." There will be some degree of hatred for that which opposes what you love.

      b) Psalm 119—"Through thy precepts I get understanding; therefore, I hate every false way. . . . I hate vain thoughts, but thy law do I love. . . . I esteem all thy precepts concerning all things to be right, and I hate every false way. . . . I hate and abhor lying, but thy law do I love" (vv. 104, 113, 128, 163). Whenever you commit yourself totally to something, you resent anything that would violate it. That is why God can be a God of love and a God of hate at the same time.

What Does God Hate?

Proverbs 6:17-19 lists seven things that God hates. In a Hebrew idiom used for emphasis, Solomon said, "These six things doth the Lord hate; yea, seven are an abomination unto him."

1. A proud look

    Pride is manifested in lofty eyes, which is the literal Hebrew meaning of that phrase. Someone who is prideful has his nose in the air and his eyes uplifted. When pride fills the heart, it is reflected in one's mannerisms. God hates people who disdain everyone and everything else. The sin of pride is probably listed first because it is the root of all disobedience and rebellion against God (Rom. 1:22).

2. A lying tongue

    God is a God of truth, who cannot lie (Heb. 6:18). That He loves truth and hates lying is illustrated in the account of Ananias and Sapphira, who lied to the Holy Spirit (Acts 5:1-11). God took their lives as an example to the early church of His holiness.

3. Murderous hands

    Verse 17 says that God hates "hands that shed innocent blood." God hates people with murderous, cruel dispositions, who will kill rather than be denied or frustrated in what they want. God hates murder because He created life and established its sanctity. Therefore God ordained that when someone takes a life, he should pay with his own life (Gen. 9:6).

4. A wicked heart

    God hates "an heart that deviseth wicked imaginations" (v. 18). It's bad enough for a person to do evil, but it's even worse when he plans at great length on how to do it. A wicked heart is the devil's workshop for devising new ways of sinning.

5. Mischievous feet

    God also hates "feet that are swift in running to mischief" (v. 18). The difference between this and normal sinning is that normal sinning is described in the Bible as a falling or a tripping. But the mischievous person purposely runs as fast as he can—he's in a hurry to sin.

6. A false witness

Another thing God hates is "a false witness that speaketh lies" (v. 19). God hates people who put the blame on an innocent party. David, Jesus, and Paul experienced accusations by false witnesses (Ps. 27:12; Matt. 26:59-61; Acts 25:7-8). Bearing false witness obstructs justice, destroys reputations, and even destroys lives in some cases.

7. A devisive spirit

Verse 19 says that God also hates the person who "soweth discord among brethren." Troublemakers create divisions where there should be unity.

The things God hates are in direct opposition to the things He loves: truth, goodness, and unity. Because He loves men to worship Him in truth, He hates idolatry and hypocritical religion. His hatred is the antithesis of His love.

B. The Analysis of the Epistle's Context

The epistle of 1 John introduces something else that God hates. First John 2:15 says there is a love that God hates: "Love not the world, neither the things that are in the world. If any man love the world, the love of the Father is not in him." God hates the love of the world and the things that are in it.

1. The thematic context

   a) Surveyed

   One of John's purposes in his letter is to distinguish the true Christian from the false Christian. He wants to show who is truly a believer and who is not. His Christian readers had been infiltrated with false teachers, which he called "antichrists" in 2:18. Evidently, the people were having a hard time figuring out who were truly saved and whose teaching they should follow. Therefore, throughout the letter he gives them some tests by which they can evaluate whether a person is a Christian or not. These tests fall into two categories: the doctrinal test (confessing sin and Christ) and the moral test (obeying God and loving the brethren). John returns to the doctrinal test (which he began in chapter 1) at the end of chapter 2, where he introduces the doctrinal test regarding Christ: "Who is a liar but he that denieth that Jesus is the Christ?. . . . Whosoever denieth the Son, the same hath not the Father; he that confesseth the Son hath the Father also" (vv. 22-23).

b) Specified

In the first half of chapter 2, John interjects the moral test of obedience and love. The moral test of love has three parts, each of which helps determine who is a Christian by identifying the objects of a person's love. First John 2:5 says, "Whosoever keepeth his word, in him verily is the love of God perfected." The first requirement for a Christian is that he loves God. The second requirement is that he "loveth his brother" (v. 10). The third is found in verse 15: "Love not the world." The love of the world is diametrically opposed to the first requirement of loving God. The apostle John is saying that a true Christian does not continue to habitually love the world. That kind of love is inconsistent with Christianity. It does not characterize the lives of Christians.

c) Supported

(1) 1 John 4:5-6—"They are of the world [unsaved]; therefore speak they of the world, and the world heareth them. We are of God." Christians are not of the world. Their citizenship has been transferred to heaven (Phil. 3:20).

(2) 1 John 5:4-5—"Whatever is born of God overcometh the world; and this is the victory that overcometh the world, even our faith. Who is he that overcometh the world, but he that believeth that Jesus is the Son of God?" A Christian has overcome the world and is no longer in love with it.

(3) John 15:18-19—Jesus said to His disciples, "If the world hate you, ye know that it hated me before it hated you. If ye were of the world, the world would love its own; but because ye are not of the world, but I have chosen you out of the world, therefore the world hateth you." Christians do not have a love relationship with the world: It hates us, and we hate it. It is the ungodly system of the world, however—not individual people—that we are to hate.

22

(4) Colossians 1:12-13—When we were saved, the Father made us "partakers of the inheritance of the saints in light; who hath delivered us from the power of darkness, and hath translated us into the kingdom of his dear Son." Our citizenship has been transferred from this world to heaven. Our manner of life is not earthly; it is heavenly.

(5) James 4:4—"Ye adulterers and adulteresses, know ye not that the friendship of the world is enmity with God? Whosoever, therefore, will be a friend of the world is the enemy of God." Christians are not enemies of God but His friends. Jesus said to His disciples, "Henceforth I call you not servants. . . . I have called you friends" (John 15:15). More than that, "we are the children of God" (Rom. 8:16)—certainly not His enemies. Romans 5:1 says that "we have made peace with God." We are no longer enemies of God. We do not love the world, because loving the world would make us enemies of God, which is inconsistent with our nature.

If you need to know whether someone is a Christian, determine if he loves God and other Christians but not the world. It may sometimes seem that Christians love the world, while failing to fully love God and His children. But remember, we're not talking about legal obedience; we're talking about gracious obedience, which allows for our failings and misdirected love. The pattern of a Christian's life is to love God, not the world. However, there are times when, even though we don't love the world, we flirt with it. And that is where grace is applied. Ideally, we obey God. Yet even though we fail from time to time, we maintain a spirit of obedience, because Christ's sacrifice for sin has already graciously paid the penalty for our sins. The pattern of a Christian's life is not to love the world but to love God. Since God and the world are at odds, you can't love both.

2. The historical context

    a) Examined

    The apostle John directed his thoughts at a particular problem: Gnosticism. Gnostic teachers were claiming to be Christians. John asks in his letter, "Do they confess sin? Do they confess Jesus Christ as God in human flesh? Do they obey the law of God? Do they love God and the brethren?" The answer to all those questions is no. One thing they did do, however, was to love the world's system. The Gnostics had infiltrated the church and propagated worldly philosophy. They falsely believed that true spirituality was only available to those who possessed a special knowledge. Their pursuit of worldly knowledge (Gk., *gnōsis*) caused them to be called Gnostics. Their system of philosophy was just as worldly as their system of morality.

b) Exemplified

Second Timothy 3:2-7 seems to describe Gnostic philosophy. Timothy may have been in a situation where Gnostics were very influential. In fact, many commentators believe Paul's warning to Timothy refers to the same Gnostics that John addresses in his letter. Paul wrote, "Men shall be lovers of their own selves, covetous, boasters, proud, blasphemers, disobedient to parents, unthankful, unholy, without natural affection, trucebreakers, false accusers, incontinent, fierce, despisers of those that are good, traitors, heady, high-minded, lovers of pleasures more than lovers of God, having a form of godliness, but denying the power of it; from such turn away. For of this sort are they who creep into houses, and lead captive silly women laden with sins, led away with various lusts, ever learning, and never able to come to the knowledge of the truth." There isn't a more fitting description of Gnostics than that passage.

God hates the things that characterized the Gnostics. Although the Gnostics claimed to be Christians, they focused on the world's philosophy and immorality. That is why John said they weren't to be in the fellowship. They actually loved the world. Therefore, the Gnostics failed the third phase of John's moral test. John helped his readers identify who was really saved so they could avoid teachers who would attempt to deceive them.

C. The Application to Modern Christians

John's imperative to his readers to stop loving the world is also an exhortation to us today. There are times when

Christians flirt with the world's system. If Christians are not to love the world, then we must submit to that truth. The Bible says that Christians should confess their sin. That doesn't necessarily mean every believer is faithful in confessing his sins. We have to be exhorted to do what every Christian should be doing. The Bible also says that Christians obey God's Word. Rather than merely hoping for obedience, they must activate their wills to obey. Similarly, the Bible says that Christians will love their brothers. Although that is an accurate description of Christians, there still need to be exhortations to love the brethren (1 Pet. 4:8). And even though the Bible indicates that a Christian will not love the world, we still need the Holy Spirit's exhortation to stop loving the world. When our lives become inconsistent with who we are, we need to activate our wills to become what we should be. We need to learn what God expects of Christians and act accordingly. If you're a Christian, you will confess your sin, but it's possible you're not doing that as faithfully as you ought to. You will obey God and love the brethren, but it's possible you're not being as faithful as you ought to be in those areas either. And if you're a Christian, you will not love the world; you will love God instead. However, it's possible that you are flirting with the world and attaching yourself to some of its attractions. When that happens, you are cleansed by Christ's sacrifice on the cross. Although Christians do not habitually love the world, they must still be careful not to love the world at all.

Lesson

First John 2:12-17 gives four reasons why Christians don't love the world:

I. BECAUSE OF WHAT THE WORLD IS (v. 15)

The word "world" is used six times in the immediate context. Verses 15-17 say, "Love not the world, neither the things that are in the world. If any man love the world, the love of the Father is not in him. For all that is in the world . . . is not of the Father, but is of the world. And the world passeth away."

A. The Definition of the World

What does John mean by the term "world"? The Greek word for "world" is *kosmos*. It has three basic meanings:

1. The earth

Kosmos is used to refer to the physical world of mountains, water bodies, plant and animal life, and all the other things that are part of God's creation on this planet. Paul uses *kosmos* that way in Acts 17:24, where he says it was "God, who made the world and all things in it." Paul was talking about the created loveliness of God's wonderful world. Is John saying that we are not to admire the beauty of the mountains, rivers, seas, and sky? No. Psalm 19 tells us that God's creation reveals His glory. Verses 1-2 say, "The heavens declare the glory of God, and the firmament showeth his handiwork. Day unto day uttereth speech, and night unto night showeth knowledge." God has created the heavenly bodies that we might know Him and see His beauty. If you read Psalm 104, you will find the psalmist's sense of awe at the beauty of God's world. We are to love the world that God has created. In fact, Christians ought to be the supreme ecologists. How can a humanistic unbeliever admire scenery that he thinks is only an accident?

We are to love the earth because God created it, and He made it for our enjoyment. If you ever had a kindergartner bring home a big mess on a piece of paper, you admired it, even though you may not have known what it was. You may have even plastered such cherished works of art all over your refrigerator. They mean something to us because they were created by someone we love. Whenever someone gives you a gift that he's made with his own hands, it carries a special meaning. We have the right to love the earth because it's the product of the very God that we love. God isn't telling us in 1 John not to love His creation.

2. The human race

    Kosmos can also refer to the world of people—humanity. That is how it is used in John 3:16: "God so loved the world." Jesus wasn't talking about the mountains and the bodies of water; He was talking about people. God loves all the people in the world. *Kosmos* is used in both ways in John 1:10: "He was in the [physical] world, and the [physical] world was made by him, and the [human] world knew him not."

    Christians are also to love the human world. God loves all men equally with no respect of persons, and we're to love the world as God loves it. We're to "do good unto all men, especially unto them who are of the household of faith" (Gal. 6:10). We are to extend the love of Christ to every man. We're not to hate the people of the world because God loves them and sent His Son to die for them.

3. The evil system

Kosmos also refers to the invisible spiritual system of evil. First John 2:15 tells us that we're not to love that evil system or the features of that system. The world's system is opposed to God.

The English language often uses the word *world* in the sense of a system. When we speak of the world of sports, the world of politics, or the world of medicine, we refer to systems of ideas, activities, and purposes that relate to a specific area of society. Hence, "the world" can also refer to Satan's ideas, activities, and purposes as they are manifested on earth. Because the satanic world system is opposed to God, there is no way you can love it and God. John says, "Love not the world, neither the things that are in the world. If any man love the world, the love of the Father is not in him" (1 John 2:15). Those two loves are antithetical.

B. The Description of the World

1. Its prince

   a) 1 John 5:19—"We know that we [Christians] are of God, and the whole world lieth in wickedness" [lit., "the wicked one"]. Christians belong to God, but the world's evil system belongs to Satan. The kingdom of God and the kingdom of Satan are incompatible.

   b) 1 John 4:4—"Ye are of God, little children, and have overcome them, because greater is he that is in you, than he that is in the world." God, who indwells us, is greater than Satan, who operates in the world. That is why a Christian loves God and hates the world's system. It's sad that the system we hate sometimes entangles us in a struggle with worldliness.

   Worldliness isn't necessarily what you do, as much it is what you think. You can do nothing but still have worldly desires. You may say, "I don't do any worldly things, but I sure would like to!" Worldliness is primarily living to experience the world's passing pleasures.

27

    c) John 12:31—The world's evil system is run by Satan, who is called "the prince of this world."

    d) Ephesians 6:11-12—Paul tells us that Satan and his demons work wickedness in the spiritual realm.

2. Its people

    a) Luke 16:8—Satan traps people in his evil system. In fact, all unsaved people are a part of the spiritual system that is against God. Jesus referred to unsaved people as "the children of this world" (KJV). Without knowing it, unbelievers are part of Satan's evil system.

    b) Philippians 3:20—"Our citizenship is in heaven" even though we live on earth. Believers are not subjects of the world's system.

    c) 1 John 4:3—"Every spirit that confesseth not that Jesus Christ is come in the flesh is not of God; and this is that spirit of antichrist, of which ye have heard that it should come, and even now already is it in the world." The spirit of antichrist is already a part of the world's evil system, which is preparing for an ultimate antichrist. The world is literally anti-Christ. If you're a Christian, you are pro-Christ. There is no harmony between the two.

    d) 1 John 4:1—"Believe not every spirit, but test the spirits whether they are of God; because many false prophets are gone out into the world." The world is inundated with false teachers.

    e) 1 John 3:1—"Behold, what manner of love the Father hath bestowed upon us, that we should be called the children of God; therefore, the world knoweth us not." The world's system can't relate to Christians. Non-Christians don't understand our relationship to God. Our world views are diametrically opposed to each other. Christians are in love with the Father, the Son, and the Spirit. The people in the world blindly follow Satan and are in love with themselves.

    f) John 17:6—Jesus said that His disciples had been chosen out of the world.

    g) Colossians 1:13—God has "translated us into the kingdom of his dear Son." Christians exist in a heavenly realm (cf. Eph. 2:6).

h) 1 John 3:13—"Marvel not, my brethren, if the world hate you." Don't be surprised when unbelievers hate what you stand for. Christians are too different for them to handle.

i) 1 John 4:5-6—"They are of the world; therefore speak they of the world, and the world heareth them. We are of God. He that knoweth God heareth us; he that is not of God heareth not us." The world listens to false prophets only. When unbelievers get upset with what I have preached, I am not surprised.

In the World, but Not of It

Although Christians have been chosen out of the world, we still rub shoulders with it. That's inevitable. Living the Christian life involves carefully interacting with the world but not being submerged in it. When a boat is in the water, there's no problem. But when the water is in the boat, you've got problems. It's all right for a Christian to be in the world, but it's not very good for the world to be in the Christian. We exist in the sphere of the world, but we don't let it overcome us. Because we belong to God, we operate in a different dimension. That doesn't mean, however, that we fail to reach into Satan's domain and try to rescue his subjects.

Why Should Christians Not Love the World?

1. It opposes God

   The very nature of the world should keep Christians from loving it. How could you love a world that hates Jesus? Could you love a system that attempts to defile everything God stands for? Could you be a part of that which is in direct opposition to God? Would you be a part of what Satan runs and his demons administer? Jesus implied that the world's system is damned when He said, "Woe unto the world because of offenses" (Matt. 18:7).

2. It is spiritually dead

   Christians can't have anything to do with the world because it is spiritually dead and cannot receive the Holy Spirit (John 14:17). In John 17:9 Jesus says to the Father, "I pray for [the disciples]; I pray not for the world."

3. Jesus died to deliver us from it

In Galatians 1:4 the apostle Paul says that Jesus "gave himself for our sins, that he might deliver us from this present evil world" (KJV).

4. It is morally polluted

Second Peter 2:20 mentions "the pollutions of the world." Just a cursory look at society will reveal that it is hostile to godliness and dominated by carnal ambition, pride, greed, self-pleasure, and evil desires. Its opinions are wrong, its aims are selfish, its pleasures are sinful, its influence is demoralizing, its politics are corrupt, its honors are empty, its smiles are fake, and its love is fickle. It's a system of rebellion against God that's run by Satan. Christians are not a part of the world's evil system and should never love it.

5. It distracts us from loving God

Love is the supreme affection. When you love someone, you are committing yourself to that person. No woman comes to the place where she tells two men, "I love both of you equally." Rather she might say, "I can't decide which one I love more." By its very definition, love knows no rivals. Love gives its object first place. To love the world is to give that system first place. If a Christian gave the world first place, that would be the antithesis of what his life should be dedicated to. That's why John says at the end of verse 15, "If any man love the world, the love of the Father is not in him." We do not love the world because it is the enemy of God.

Conclusion

There are many things about the world's system that entice us. The lust of the flesh (v. 16) affects the area of sexual gratification. Sexual immorality is rampant on television and other kinds of entertainment. It is difficult to avoid being inundated with the world's emphasis on the lust of the flesh. Another common lust of the flesh in our society is gluttony. There are countless commercials about fast food restaurants. Food isn't only for the purpose of sustenance any longer—it's entertainment. You don't necessarily go out to eat because the food's good; you go because you like the atmosphere. It's hard to avoid gluttony, which isn't just being overweight; it's eating for the sake of fulfilling the lust of your flesh beyond the point of your body's need.

There are many things like those that are hard to resist. Maybe the lust of the eyes (v. 16) is a problem as you look around and see something new and wonderful that causes you to want it badly. Maybe pride is a problem. I heard a TV commercial state that you ought to have a certain product because of what your neighbors would say.

If you're a Christian and you really don't love the world but find that the sin in you is drawing you to worldly affections, you should confess that to Christ. Spend some time praying to the Lord and reading about Him until you fall more in love with Him. The more you love Him, the less you'll love the things that would push aside godly priorities in your life. We don't love the world because of what it is—the enemy of all that we are and all that we love.

Focusing on the Facts

1. What attribute of God does the apostle John emphasize in his first letter (see p. 19)?
2. What other divine response is inseparable from God's love? Explain (see p. 19).
3. Why most likely is the sin of pride listed first in the list of things God hates (Prov. 6:17; see p. 20)?
4. Identify one of the purposes of John's letter (see p. 21).
5. What are the three parts of the test of obedience and love (see p. 22)?
6. What does a Christian's faith enable him to do in relation to the world, according to 1 John 5:4-5 (see p. 22)?
7. What does James 4:4 call men and women who redirect their devotion from God to the world (see p. 23)?
8. Explain the particular problem of Gnosticism that the apostle Paul was writing against (see pp. 23-24).
9. What are the three basic meanings for the Greek term for "world" in the New Testament (see pp. 25-27)?
10. What two forms of the world are Christians supposed to love? Explain (see pp. 25-27).
11. Who rules the world's system? Support your answer with Scripture (see pp. 27-28).
12. Even though Christians live on earth, where is their citizenship (Phil. 3:20; see p. 28)?
13. Explain how a boat in water can illustrate the Christian in the world (see p. 29).
14. Why did Jesus give "himself for our sins," according to Galatians 1:4 (see pp. 29-30)?
15. What are some elements of the lust of the flesh that entice us in our society (see pp. 30-31)?
16. How can a Christian fall more in love with Jesus than he is with the world (see p. 31)?

Pondering the Principles

1. Look back at the seven things said to be things God hates (Prov. 6:17-19; see pp. 20). If you are a Christian, none of those things should be consistently present in your life. However, you may struggle with some of them from time to time. Analyze your life with regard to each of those sins. Pray that you would submit your will to God's in any area that poses a potential threat. Look up the following verses to determine the New Testament counterpart of those sins: Luke 6:31-37; Ephesians 4:15; 4:25; Philippians 2:2; 2 Timothy 2:22; Hebrews 12:1, 13-14; James 4:10.

2. Meditate on Matthew 19:16-30. Jesus confronted a rich young ruler about what stood between him and his complete devotion to God—his wealth. Is there any attraction of the world that prevents you from following Christ? Memorize James 4:4: "Do you not know that friendship with the world is hostility toward God? Therefore whoever wishes to be a friend of the world makes himself an enemy of God" (NASB*).

3. The world's system is so morally polluted that it is difficult to function in society without being tempted to indulge in "the passing pleasures of sin" (Heb. 11:25, NASB). Meditate on Hebrews 12:1-15. What are Christians told to lay aside in the race of life? Why? Whom are we to focus on as we run? Training in righteousness is difficult, but it is necessary for the Christian who is enlisted in active duty against the world's system and the demonic forces that oppose God. What do you need to do to strengthen yourself as you run the race toward righteousness? Run with endurance as you hurdle the obstacles of the world. Don't ever lose sight of who you are and where you are headed.

3
The Love God Hates—
Part 2

Outline

Introduction

Review
I. Because of What the World Is (v. 15)

Lesson
II. Because of Who Christians Are (vv. 12-14)
   A. The Mercy Extended Towards God's Children (v. 12)
      1. Stated
      2. Supported
   B. The Maturing Process of God's Children (vv. 13-14)
      1. Explaining spiritual maturity
         a) Mark 4:28
         b) John 21:15-16
         c) Romans 14:1; 15:1
      2. Encouraging spiritual maturity
      3. Examining spiritual maturity
         a) Little children (v. 13c)
            (1) Their character explained
            (2) Their character exemplified
               (a) 1 Corinthians 3:1
               (b) Ephesians 4:14
               (c) Matthew 11:25
         b) Young men (vv. 13b, 14b)
            (1) Their understanding of Scripture
            (2) Their use of strength
            (3) Their understanding of Satan
               (a) His strategy stated
               (b) His strategy supported
         c) Spiritual fathers (vv. 13a, 14a)

Conclusion
A. The Injunctions for Spiritual Growth
B. The Ingredients for Spiritual Growth
1. God's Word
2. Holy living

Introduction

First John 2:12-17 discusses the subject of love. However, it isn't the kind of love that is honoring to God; rather it is a love that He hates. The apostle John says, "Love not the world, neither the things that are in the world. If any man love the world, the love of the Father is not in him" (v. 15). The meaning of the term "world" in this context refers to the system of evil that dominates the earth. Christians are not to love that system because it is inconsistent with their love for the Father. First John 5:19 says that the whole world lies in control of the wicked one. It conveys the picture of a nurse cradling a child. The whole world is cradled in the arms of Satan. Christians are not citizens of this world; we are citizens of heaven (Phil. 3:20). Although we exist in the satanically inspired system that dominates man's society, we are not to love it because it is corrupt (2 Pet. 1:4) and godless (1 John 2:16).

One of the problems that the church continually faces is determining who speaks truth and who distorts truth. John's epistle gives some tests for telling the true from the false. You can tell a true Christian from a false one by what he believes and by what he does. The doctrinal test has two parts: confessing sin and confessing Christ. The moral test also has two parts: obedience and love. A true Christian will love God and fellow Christians, but he will not love the world, because it is impossible for a true Christian to continually be in love with a satanic system that opposes God. A person must choose sides. Jesus said, "He that is not with me is against me" (Matt. 12:30). He also said, "No man can serve two masters" (Matt. 6:24). You cannot be a spiritual schizophrenic. You cannot say, "I love God and the brethren, but I also love the world's satanic system." That's an impossibility, because you would be loving opposites.

Although true Christians do not love the world, we sometimes flirt with it. The present imperative in verse 15, which exhorts us to stop loving the world, implies that we must be diligent to become what we should be. Christians by nature and by position do not habitually love the world's system—we aren't even to flirt with it. The Old Testament says: "Choose you this day whom ye will serve" (Josh. 24:15).

Review

John gives four reasons here for not loving the world:

I. BECAUSE OF WHAT THE WORLD IS (v. 15; see pp. 25-31)

Lesson

II. BECAUSE OF WHO CHRISTIANS ARE (vv. 12-14)

The second reason Christians do not love the world is that we are God's family. Verse 15 says, "If any man love the world, the love of the Father is not in him." Those two loves are mutually exclusive. John 8 illustrates why. The Pharisees said to Jesus, "Abraham is our father. Jesus saith unto them, If ye were Abraham's children, ye would do the works of Abraham. But now ye seek to kill me, a man that hath told you the truth, which I have heard of God; this did not Abraham. Ye do the deeds of your father. . . . Ye are of your father the devil" (vv. 39-41, 44). The Pharisees claimed to be the children of Abraham, but they didn't act like Abraham.

There are two families in the world: the family of God and the family of Satan. We do not believe in the fatherhood of God or the brotherhood of man—that God is everyone's father and that all men are brothers. Men are either children of God or of Satan. As Christians, we do not love the world because we are the family of God. First John 2:12-14 says, "I write unto you, little children, because your sins are forgiven you for his name's sake. I write unto you, fathers, because ye have known him that is from the beginning. I write unto you, young men, because ye have overcome the wicked one. I write unto you, little children, because ye have known the Father. I have written unto you, fathers, because ye have known him that is from the beginning. I have written unto you, young men, because ye are strong, and the word of God abideth in you, and ye have overcome the wicked one." John describes the different kinds of believers in the family of God. Some are spiritual babies, some are young men, and some are fathers, but we are all His children. Therefore, because I'm a child of God, I don't love Satan's system or give my allegiance to him. John speaks about the family of God and the different levels of maturity that His children have. True Christians are forgiven, they know God, and they have overcome Satan's system. The very nature of the family allows no possibility of loving God and the satanic system simultaneously.

A. The Mercy Extended Towards God's Children (v. 12)

"I write unto you, little children (Gk., *teknia*), because your sins are forgiven you for his name's sake."

1. Stated

The term *teknia* has a general meaning of "born ones" without designation of age. John is acknowledging that his readers are all the offspring of God. As His children, their sins are forgiven for His name's sake. That is a fantastic statement. Our sins are not forgiven because we have asked them to be forgiven—although in a sense that's true. They are primarily forgiven because of God's name. In other words, God forgave us because that act of mercy glorified Him. It was for the sake of His name that He forgave you and me. It wasn't because we deserved it. The reason you and I are saved is because God has a merciful nature. God chose to display His mercy, and we are simply the benefactors.

God desires to demonstrate His glory. If you understand that, then you will understand a primary emphasis of Scripture. God made man to be a vehicle of His glory. He wants to put His attributes on display. When you stand up as a graciously forgiven sinner, the world can recognize that God is gracious and forgiving. It honors God to redeem you. In fact, Ephesians 3:10 says He has put the church on display before the angels that the angels might give Him praise for His wisdom. God's glory is a foundational reason for all that He does. Let's examine some passages that demonstrate God's desire to display His mercy.

2. Supported

a) Micah 7:18-19—The prophet asks the rhetorical question "Who is a God like unto thee, who pardoneth iniquity, and passeth by the transgression of the remnant of his heritage? He retaineth not his anger forever, because he delighteth in mercy. He will turn again; he will have compassion upon us; he will subdue our iniquities; and thou wilt cast all their sins into the depths of the sea." What a pardoning God! He pardons sin to display His merciful character.

b) Psalm 32:2—David said, "Blessed is the man unto whom the Lord imputeth not iniquity."

c) Psalm 86:5—"Thou, Lord, art good, and ready to forgive, and plenteous in mercy unto all those who call upon thee." The criterion for receiving mercy is calling upon the Lord. God is a God of forgiveness. He has always been that way, even though there are people who teach that the God of the Old Testament is different from the God of the New Testament. They fail to see the abundant evidence of God's grace in the Old Testament.

d) Isaiah 43:25—God said of Himself, "I, even I, am he who blotteth out thy transgressions for mine own sake, and will not remember thy sins." The primary reason God forgave you was not for you; it was for Him. The main theme of the universe is that its Creator is to be glorified. We need a lofty picture of our great, merciful God, who pardons that He might display His grace to the world.

e) Luke 24:47—Jesus commissioned His disciples that "repentance and [forgiveness] of sins should be preached in his name among all nations."

f) Ephesians 1:4-6—The Father has "chosen us in him before the foundation of the world . . . having predestinated us . . . to the praise of the glory of his grace."

g) Psalm 25:11—"For thy name's sake, O Lord, pardon mine iniquity." David said, "Lord, I want You to pardon my sin, not for my sake but for Yours." Have you ever prayed like that?

Praying the Perfect Prayer

Have you ever prayed, "Lord, save so-and-so that it might be a glory to Your name"; or, "Lord, so-and-so is sick; heal him for Your glory"; or, "Lord, so-and-so is sick and may die. Do whatever gives You the most glory"? That's the way to pray. When we pray for our sake, we reverse the priorities. If you always pray for what you want, you'll never be able to pray according to the will of God because you won't be interested in it. But when you pray, "Do whatever gives You glory, God," you really are praying the right way. You've got to care about the glory of God first. Sometimes that isn't easy because we want so many other things. If you pray just for yourself, you are selfish and don't understand the importance of God's glory. Jesus said,

"If ye shall ask anything in my name, I will do it" (John 14:14). In other words, "If you ask anything for the sake of My name—anything that will give Me glory—I'll do it." So your prayers should be, "Father, do this because I believe it will be for the glory of Christ." A person who consistently prays that way reveals his spiritual maturity. Sometimes it's difficult not to pray for ourselves, and I'm sure God understands that. But in the back of our minds we must remember that everything is for His glory. If you're having trouble accepting that, then you'll have trouble attaining spiritual maturity.

> *h)* Psalm 79:8—"Remember not against us former iniquities; let thy tender mercies speedily meet us; for we are brought very low. Help us, O God of our salvation, for the glory of thy name; and deliver us, and purge away our sins, for thy name's sake."
>
> *i)* Psalm 106:8—"Nevertheless, he saved them for his name's sake, that he might make his mighty power to be known." The Lord saved Israel, and He saves us to display His glory to the rest of the world.
>
> *j)* Psalm 109:21—David knew how to pray. He said, "Do thou for me, O God the Lord, for thy name's sake; because thy mercy is good, deliver thou me."
>
> *k)* Jeremiah 14:7—"O Lord, though our iniquities testify against us, do it for thy name's sake." When you care more about God's glory than you do about yourself, that's maturity.
>
> *l)* Isaiah 48:9, 11—"For my name's sake will I defer mine anger, and for my praise will I refrain for thee, that I cut thee not off. . . . For mine own sake, even for mine own sake, will I do it."

The family of God has been forgiven. I'm not worried about the effectiveness of God's forgiveness because He forgives us for His sake, not mine. People say, "I wonder if He's forgiving me." If He designs to forgive you for His sake, accept His graciousness. You didn't earn His forgiveness, and you can't earn it now. He does it for His own sake. As members of God's family, we have been forgiven. How then could we ever love that which is part of the world's system?

B. The Maturing Process of God's Children (vv. 13-14)

   1. Explaining spiritual maturity

The Bible teaches that there are levels of spiritual maturity. Not all Christians are at the same level; otherwise Peter wouldn't have exhorted us to "grow in grace" (2 Pet. 3:18) or to "desire the pure milk of the word, that ye may grow by it" (1 Pet. 2:2). Let's see how the process of maturity is illustrated in Scripture.

a) Mark 4:28—Jesus used the analogy of the growth stages of grain to indicate the mystery of spiritual growth: "For the earth bringeth forth fruit of itself: first the blade, then the ear, after that the full grain in the ear."

b) John 21:15-16—When questioning the commitment of Peter's love for Him, Jesus requested him to feed not only His lambs but His sheep as well. The Lord recognized at least two different levels of spiritual growth: mature sheep and little lambs. I believe that any preacher who is going to feed his flock has got to be aware that there are lambs as well as sheep in his congregation. He should always have something in his message for both groups.

c) Romans 14:1; 15:1—Paul's discussion of the weaker brother indicates different levels of spiritual maturity.

Spirituality is not the same thing as maturity. Spirituality is a momentary absolute; maturity is a process. A spiritual Christian walks in the Spirit, while a carnal Christian walks in the flesh. Can you be a spiritual Christian at any point in your growth? Sure you can. You can also lose your spirituality by walking in the flesh. Even someone who gets to the level of a spiritual father could still act in the flesh. Spirituality depends on whether at any given moment a Christian is yielded to the Holy Spirit. In contrast, maturity is the process of becoming more spiritual and less carnal. The maturing process can occur only in the context of spirituality. For example, a spiritual babe, who knows only the ABC's of Christianity, can become a spiritual young man as he walks in the Spirit. As soon as he acts in the flesh, his growth reaches a plateau. But as he yields to the Spirit, he begins to grow again. You can grow only when you allow God to work through you.

2. Encouraging spiritual maturity

All spiritual babes do not automatically become young men, and young men do not automatically become fathers. You say, "I may be a spiritual baby now, but give me a couple of years, and I'll be a young man." Spiritual maturity isn't solely a matter of time. There are some Christians who never progress past the stage of spiritual infancy as a result of death, backsliding, or failure to study the Word. However, all spiritual babes should become young men and fathers. Paul says in Ephesians 4:14, "Be no more children, tossed to and fro, and carried about with every wind of doctrine, by the sleight of men, and cunning craftiness, by which they lie in wait to deceive." If you are a Christian who isn't growing, you are contradicting the very essence of what the Lord expects of you. First Corinthians 14:20 says, "Brethren, be not children in understanding." In our understanding, we are to be mature men. However, the level of a person's spiritual growth has very little to do with age.

3. Examining spiritual maturity

   a) Little children (v. 13*c*)

      "I write unto you, little children, because ye have known the Father."

      (1) Their character explained

         All Christians start as spiritual children. They must first be born into God's family. The Greek word for "children" in verse 13 is *paidia*, not *teknia*, which is used in verse 12 to refer to people who are born of God (who become Christians). *Paidia*, however, refers to infants and is associated with ignorance. Our English word *pedagogy*, which involves instruction, has that Greek term as its root. These children are spiritually uninstructed. Their understanding is limited to the basics of salvation: They know the Father. In the natural realm, the first thing a baby discovers is its parents. "Mama" and "Dada" are some of the first words babies can say. Similarly, in the spiritual realm, the distinguishing characteristic of a baby Christian is his acknowledgement of God as his heavenly Father. He expresses his attachment to God. He delights in God and depends on Him. According to Paul in Galatians 4:6 and Romans 8:15, the spiritual babe addresses God as "Abba," (an Aramaic equivalent of "daddy").

Invariably little children are regulated by their affections, not by their understanding. They don't reason things out. They delight in their experiences. They're quickly excited and easily afraid. In the same way, spiritual children wonder if they're really saved and if Satan and his demons can have any affect on them. If they hear about prophecy, they're worried about whether they are going to get taken in the rapture. They struggle with those kinds of fears because they express their relationship to God on an emotional basis rather than a rational one. Throughout the Bible, when the concept of children is used in a spiritual sense, it refers to spiritual ignorance.

(2) Their character exemplified

(a) 1 Corinthians 3:1—"I, brethren, could not speak unto you as spiritual, but as unto carnal, even as unto babes [Gk., *nēpeon*] in Christ. I have fed you with milk, and not with solid food; for to this time ye were not able to bear it." Because the Corinthians were ignorant of deeper spiritual truths, Paul could teach them only basic things. The reason they stayed as infants is that they were carnal. Spiritual growth occurs only when a Christian walks in the Spirit.

(b) Ephesians 4:14—Christians who are little children spiritually are saved, but they are easily swept away by false doctrine because of their limited understanding of true doctrine. Invariably, it's the spiritual infants who get sucked into the cults with their doctrinal heresies.

(c) Matthew 11:25—Jesus said, "I thank thee, O Father, Lord of heaven and earth, because thou hast hidden these things from the wise and prudent, and hast revealed them unto babes." The contrast implies that "babes" are ignorant. The disciples were naive spiritual babes.

b) Young men (vv. 13*b*, 14*b*)

"I write unto you, young men, because ye have overcome the wicked one. . . . I have written unto you, young men, because ye are strong, and the word of God abideth in you, and ye have overcome the wicked one."

(1) Their understanding of Scripture

Apparently, John addresses the different spiritual levels of Christians a second time for emphasis. If you're going to overcome the wicked one, who is Satan, you have to be strong. How do you get strong? By letting the Word of God abide in you. When you do that, you are a spiritual young man. A spiritual baby is ignorant, but a young man has understanding. He's no longer functioning on his emotions; he has a grasp of theology. Unfortunately, it is usually at this stage that the problem of spiritual pride appears. A spiritual young man can get to the place where he thinks he knows all the answers. That's true in the natural realm: Little children may not think they know anything, but teenagers think they know everything. Then, when you get into your late twenties, you realize you don't know as much as you once thought. No one knows as much as a teenager thinks he does. When you get to the place where you know a lot, you need to watch for the stumbling block of spiritual pride.

(2) Their use of strength

Young men are doctrinally strong. Therefore, they've overcome the wicked one. You may say, "John, I can't imagine overcoming Satan." I don't see that as a problem. In fact, I never give Satan a second thought. Even when I read a book about Satan, I don't dwell on him; I just think about what the book says in relation to what God is doing. There are some Christians who are so worried about the devil that they spend a great deal of time reading about him. But if you are a spiritual young man, you have overcome Satan. A spiritual young man no longer functions on his emotions because he knows where he stands doctrinally.

How Do You Know When You Are a Spiritual Young Man?

You know you've arrived at that level of maturity when false doctrine doesn't interest you but gets you angry. If someone asks, "What do you believe?" you are able to tell them and support your answer with Scripture. A young man has outgrown his emotions and feelings and looks to the Word for guidance. Whereas spiritual babies are primarily concerned about their own needs, a young man is not. Did you ever know of a baby that cried because his little brother or sister had a problem? No, because children are naturally self-centered. However, the concern of a spiritual young man is to learn the Word of God to become well-established in sound doctrine.

(3) Their understanding of Satan

(a) His strategy stated

But what does knowing doctrine have to do with overcoming the wicked one? Simply this: Satan operates in the area of false doctrine. If I sin, I don't say, "The devil made me do it." I don't need the devil to sin because my flesh will do that on its own. Galatians 5:19-21 tells us about the works of the flesh. Some people try to blame their sins on the demon of this or the demon of that. Although demons may be indirectly involved, the problem is our sinful flesh. Satan and his cohorts aren't running around poking people in the ribs saying, "Think a dirty thought," "Steal that lettuce," or, "Cheat on your income tax." The demonic forces have other things to do. Knowing, however, that our flesh can be activated by impulses from the world, Satan does indirectly tempt us through the world's system, which he controls.

(b) His strategy supported

i) 2 Corinthians 11:14-15—Satan disguises himself as "an angel of light" (v. 14). He is busy working (as are his servants, who similarly are "transformed as the ministers of righteousness"; v. 15) in false systems of religion. They must be busy

43

because there are so many false religions and cults in the world.

ii) Leviticus 17:7—"They shall no more offer their sacrifices unto demons, after whom they have played the harlot." Satanic activity in the area of religion isn't anything new. The Old Testament tells us that when pagan people offered sacrifices to their gods, they were actually offering sacrifices to demons.

iii) Deuteronomy 32:17—When Israel rebelliously sacrificed to false gods, "They sacrificed unto demons, not to God; to gods whom they knew not." Satan is either directly or indirectly involved in every false religion. Consequently, anyone who bows at any shrine rather than at the cross of Jesus Christ is offering himself to a demon.

iv) Psalm 106:36-37—"They served their idols, which were a snare unto them. Yea, they sacrificed their sons and their daughters unto demons." All the religions of the world, regardless of their levels of sophistication, are designed by Satan and manipulated by demons. Since Satan operates in that arena, you will overcome him when you are solid in doctrinal truth.

v) 1 Timothy 4:1—The Bible says there will be those who "depart from the faith, giving heed to seducing spirits, and doctrines of demons." False doctrine is where demons are most operative.

vi) 1 John 4:1—John warned, "Believe not every spirit, but test the spirits whether they are of God; because many false prophets are gone out into the world." Such teachers are spirits of the Antichrist (1 John 2:18).

44

vii) 1 Corinthians 10:20-21—The apostle Paul warned the Corinthians that they were trying to have fellowship with the Lord and with demons at the same time by carrying on their pagan worship. All religion that is outside of biblical Christianity is demonically influenced.

Satan disguises himself as an angel of light. That's his primary function. Therefore, when you know sound doctrine, you will overcome Satan. When you were saved, you overcame the world (1 John 5:4). When you become knowledgeable about the Word of God, you overcome Satan. The only enemy left is the flesh. Unfortunately, you have to wait until you are taken to heaven to get rid of that problem. Satan shouldn't be a problem for any spiritual young man.

c) Spiritual fathers (vv. 13a, 14a)

"I write unto you, fathers, because ye have known him that is from the beginning. . . . I have written unto you, fathers, because ye have known him that is from the beginning."

Spiritual babies delight in their experiences, and young men delight in their understanding, but fathers delight in God. It's one thing to be a spiritual young man and know the Word; it's something else to be a spiritual father and know the God behind the page. The spiritual father has plumbed the depths of the knowledge of God. He doesn't just know doctrine; he knows the God who revealed it. He may spend as much time in prayer as he does in study because he knows the Word and wants to commune with the One who is revealed in it. A spiritual father has a personal, experiential, in-depth knowledge of God. That kind of knowledge was in Paul's mind when he said, "That I may know him" (Phil. 3:10). Paul sought to plumb the depths of all that God is.

Conclusion

A. The Injunctions for Spiritual Growth

There are different levels of maturity within God's family.

Some of you are little children, some of you are young men, and some of you are fathers. Regardless of the level you are currently at, there is probably nothing more important than growing spiritually. The New Testament talks about the process of spiritual growth in many terms:

1. First Timothy 6:11 says we are to "follow after righteousness."

2. Romans 6:4 says we are to "walk in newness of life."

3. Romans 12:2 says we are to be continually transformed.

4. Second Corinthians 7:1 says we are to be "perfecting holiness."

5. Ephesians 4:15 says we are to grow up into Christ.

6. Philippians 3:14 says we are to "press toward the mark."

7. Colossians 2:7 says we are to be built up in the faith.

8. Second Peter 3:18 says we are to "grow in grace."

9. Colossians 3:16 says we are to "let the Word of Christ dwell in [us] richly."

B. The Ingredients for Spiritual Growth

Spiritual growth isn't a mystical or a psychological process. It is simply the result of two things: the Word of God and holiness. As you study the Word and walk in obedience to it in holy living, maturity takes place. There aren't any secrets. Spiritual growth is not an instantaneous gimmick.

1. God's Word

The Word of God is necessary to make you grow. That growth process is called sanctification in the New Testament. Paul says in Acts 20:32, "I commend you to God, and to the word of his grace, which is able to build you up." In 2 Timothy 3:16 he says, "All scripture is given by inspiration of God, and is profitable for doctrine, for reproof, for correction, for instruction in righteousness, that the man of God may be [mature]." Maturity comes out of the Word. There isn't any secret formula.

2. Holy living

Holiness is the second ingredient necessary for spiritual growth. You grow when you walk in the Spirit, shunning every known sin and obeying every known command. When you strive to be like Jesus Christ and yield to the Holy Spirit, spiritual fruit will be produced in you. But even holiness is a result of the Word. In John 15:3 Jesus says "Now ye are clean through the word which I have spoken unto you."

God wants His family to grow. If we are spiritual babies, let's be young men. If we're young men, let's be fathers. The Christian does not love the world because of what it is, the enemy of God—and because of who we are, the family of God.

Focusing on the Facts

1. What are the first two reasons that Christians do not love the world (see p. 35)?
2. Are all men brothers in a spiritual sense? Is God the spiritual father of all men? Explain (see p. 35).
3. What is the primary reason that the sins of God's children have been forgiven? Explain (see p. 36).
4. Why did God make man (see p. 36)?
5. What divine attribute does God display when He pardons sin (see p. 36)?
6. People who claim that the God of the Old Testament is not the same as the God of the New Testament fail to see what truth (see p. 37)?
7. Explain how the object of a Christian's prayers can reveal his level of spiritual maturity (see pp. 37-38).
8. Why shouldn't you be worried about the effectiveness of God's forgiveness (see p. 38)?
9. How does John 21:15-16 indicate that there are different levels of spiritual growth (see p. 39)?
10. Differentiate between spirituality and maturity. What does spirituality depend on? What does maturity depend on (see p. 39)?
11. Do spiritual babes automatically become young men and young men automatically become spiritual fathers? Explain (see pp. 39-40).
12. Why does Paul exhort Christians not to remain spiritual children in Ephesians 4:14 (see p. 40)?
13. To what is the understanding of spiritual children limited (see p. 40)?
14. How does a young man overcome Satan (see p. 42)?
15. What is the potential problem a spiritual young man faces (see p. 42)?
16. How do you know if you are a spiritual young man (see p. 43)?
17. Is the devil usually responsible when we sin? Explain. How does Satan tempt us to sin (see p. 43)?

18. Where do Satan and his forces concentrate their energies? Support your answer with Scripture (see pp. 43-44).
19. Once a mature Christian has already overcome the world and Satan, what is the only enemy left to conquer? When will it be fully overcome (see p. 43)?
20. Describe the characteristics of a spiritual father (see p. 45).
21. Spiritual growth is the result of what two things (see p. 46)?
22. You grow when you walk in the Spirit, _____every known_____ and every known _____(see p. 47).

Pondering the Principles

1. Read Psalm 86. Memorize verse 5. Praise the Lord for His great mercy that He has personally extended towards you.

2. What is your primary concern when you pray? Is it God's glory or your own desires? Read James 4:3. As you pray during the next week, be conscious of your motives. Aim at praying for things that are consistent with what you understand God's will to be. When we pray according to God's will, what confidence can we have, according to 1 John 5:14-15?

3. Consider Paul's statement to the Corinthians in his first letter to them: "I have fed you with milk, and not with solid food; for to this time ye were not able to bear it" (3:2). Are you sensitive to the unique backgrounds, personalities, and maturity of Christians you help to nourish spiritually? Are you demanding too much from them for their level of spiritual maturity? Should you be demanding more? Study various discipleship materials that are available from Christian bookstores and ministries. Be familiar with them so that you can give instruction that will edify believers at their particular stages of growth.

4. Spiritual growth is not easily acquired. The enemies we face (Satan, the world, and the flesh) make growing to be more like Christ a struggle. Spiritual growth requires determination and consistency. Are those two factors present in your life? Do you desire to have the deep personal knowledge of God that a spiritual father has? What are you doing to allow the Word of God to build you up? Faithfully commit yourself to obeying God's Word, and He will take you where you are and lead you to higher levels of spiritual maturity for His glory.

4
The Love God Hates—
Part 3

Outline

Introduction
A. The Reality of Satan's Reign
B. The Review of Satan's Reign
   1. False religion
   2. Crime
   3. Godless living

Review
  I. Because of What the World Is (v. 15)
 II. Because of Who Christians Are (vv. 12-14)

Lesson
III. Because of What the World Does (vv. 15-16)
   A. The Contrast of the World (v. 15)
     1. The desire of God
     2. The defilement of the world
   B. The Content of the World (v.16)
     1. The lust of the flesh
       a) Defined
       b) Delineated
         (1) Immorality
         (2) Idolatry
         (3) Interpersonal relationships
         (4) Indulgence
     2. The lust of the eyes
       a) Joshua 7:1-26
       b) 2 Samuel 11:1-17
       c) Matthew 5:27-29
       d) Job 31:1
     3. The pride of life
IV. Because of Where the World Is Going (v. 17)

49

A. Its Passing Discussed
B. Its Passing Depicted
    1. The process of deterioration
        a) 2 Thessalonians 2:7
        b) 2 Timothy 3:13
    2. The peak of destruction
        a) The setting of the scene
        b) The retribution upon the rejectors
            (1) The seals
            (2) The trumpets
        c) The end of the economy
        d) The voices of victory

Introduction

A. The Reality of Satan's Reign

The New Testament uses the term *world* in different ways. Originally the term had two basic meanings: the planet and the people. But once man rebelled against God, he forfeited his right to rule the planet God gave him to rule. In effect, man sold the title deed of the world, which fell into the control of Satan. In his short-sighted desire to be an autonomous being, man sold his birthright to the world to Satan for the knowledge of good and evil, much as Esau sold his birthright to Jacob for something to eat (Gen. 25:27-34). Adam and Eve ate of the tree, following Satan's desires. At that point, Satan gained the rulership of the world, and the term *world* took on a third meaning: the evil system, opposed to God, that now dominates this planet. The system that Satan began will continue to develop up to the time period known as the Great Tribulation.

Satan runs the world. Luke 4:6 gives us evidence of that: "The devil said to Him [Jesus], 'I will give You all this domain [of the kingdoms of the world] and its glory; for it has been handed over to me, and I give it to whomever I wish'" (NASB). The system that dominates the world is in the control of Satan. But Jesus knew that some day He would take it back as its rightful heir.

B. The Review of Satan's Reign

Genesis 4 shows us how Satan's system began to develop. Three factors characterized his system and enabled him to control the world:

1. False religion

   Satan needed to counteract the truth. So he developed lies about God, eternal destiny, and other spiritual truths. The results of those lies first appear in Genesis 4:6-7: "The Lord said unto Cain, Why art thou angry? And why is thy countenance fallen? If thou doest well, shalt thou not be accepted? And if thou doest not well, sin lieth at the door." Sin ruled over Cain because he failed to obey God. Although the Lord had apparently made it known that He required sacrifices for atonement, Cain brought the fruit of his hands—things he had grown in the field. However, Abel brought a blood sacrifice. Genesis 4 records the initial development of false religion, which is based on one thing: human works. Abel brought a sacrifice for sin, which was a picture of the final sacrifice (i.e., Christ). Cain brought his own works, which have been the continual legacy for false religions throughout the centuries. All false religions claim that man enters God's presence not on the basis of what God has done by His grace but on the basis of what man can do himself if he is good enough.

   Satan knew that if he was going to control the world's system, he would have to do it through religion, since man is a religious being. So he developed a religion that opposed God's grace and exalted man's own achievements. There are basically only two religions in the world: the religion of divine accomplishment or the religion of human achievement.

2. Crime

   Satan brought fear and bondage into man's life through crime. That began in Genesis 4:8. "Cain talked with Abel his brother: and it came to pass, when they were in the field, that Cain rose up against Abel, his brother, and slew him." Men are pitted against men. Throughout history, Satan has used crime, arguments, riots, and wars to destroy the unity that God had intended the world to have. All forms of crime are a threat against unity. Every time a person steals, covets, or destroys what is someone else's—even to the point of killing—the unity that God designed for mankind to experience disintegrates further.

3. Godless living

   Another thing that Satan brought into his system was a

pattern of godless living that operates independently of God.

Satan has developed a system in which he can captivate men. It is anti-God and anti-Christ. It is in rebellion against the truth and contradicts the divine perspective. Behind that system is Satan. He isn't directly responsible for everything that the world does, but he's behind it. For example, every time you are tempted, you are not tempted by Satan any more than every allied soldier shot in World War II on the European front was killed by Hitler—and yet Hitler was behind those deaths. In like manner, Satan is behind what's happening today in opposition to God's kingdom.

Review

First John 2:15 tells us to stop loving the system and the things that are in it; for if anyone is in love with it, his claim to love God is invalid. The system that Satan has developed is in total opposition to God. A person cannot love both. John is defining a Christian as one who loves God, rather than Satan's system. James 4:2-4 makes a similar exhortation: "Ye lust, and have not; ye kill, and desire to have, and cannot obtain; ye fight and war, yet ye have not, because ye ask not. Ye ask, and receive not, because ye ask amiss, that ye may consume it upon your lusts. Ye adulterers and adulteresses, know ye not that the friendship of the world is enmity with God? Whosoever, therefore, will be a friend of the world is the enemy of God." Love for the world and love for God are absolutely antithetical. A person cannot love both at the same time. A true Christian does not love the world. It is impossible because that is incongruous with who he is. Christians do not love the world for several reasons:

I. BECAUSE OF WHAT THE WORLD IS (v. 15; see pp. 25-31)

II. BECAUSE OF WHO CHRISTIANS ARE (vv. 12-14; see pp. 35-47)

Lesson

III. BECAUSE OF WHAT THE WORLD DOES (vv. 15-16)

    A. The Contrast of the World (v. 15)

        1. The desire of God

            "Love not the world, neither the things that are in the world. If any man love the things in the world, the love of the Father is not in him."

52

We do not love the world because of what it does. It incites to sin. The world's system is designed to tempt a person to sin. God wants to generate holiness in our lives as we become more like Jesus Christ. Satan uses the world to tempt us. Some of us are able to resist the world's temptation because of our maturity in Christ. But that does not change the evil intentions of the world, which opposes the holiness that God desires in every Christian's life.

a) 1 John 2:1—"My little children, these things write I unto you, that ye sin not." God does not want us to sin.

b) Ephesians 2:10—"We are his workmanship, created in Christ Jesus unto good works, which God hath before ordained that we should walk in them."

c) Romans 6:17-18—"God be thanked, that whereas ye were the servants of sin, ye have obeyed from the heart that form of doctrine which was delivered you. Being, then, made free from sin, ye became the servants of righteousness." A Christian is a servant of righteousness. Having been forgiven, he serves a new Master.

d) 2 Corinthians 6:14-17—The apostle Paul said, "Be ye not unequally yoked together with unbelievers; for what fellowship hath righteousness with unrighteousness? And what communion hath light with darkness? And what concord hath Christ with [Satan]? Or what part hath he that believeth with an [unbeliever]? And what agreement hath the temple of God with idols? . . . Wherefore, come out from among them, and be ye separate, saith the Lord, and touch not the unclean thing; and I will receive you." God desires that we be separate from sin.

e) 2 Corinthians 7:1—"Having, therefore, these promises, dearly beloved, let us cleanse ourselves from all filthiness of the flesh and spirit, perfecting holiness." God's desire is that the believer live by His righteous standards.

f) Philippians 2:15—We are to be "blameless and harmless, children of God, without rebuke, in the midst of a crooked and perverse nation, among whom [we] shine as lights in the world." We should live in such a way that the watching world cannot accuse our life-style.

g) 1 Thessalonians 3:12-13—"The Lord make you to increase and abound in love one toward another, and toward all men, even as we do toward you, to the end he may establish your hearts unblamable in holiness."

h) 1 Thessalonians 4:7—"For God hath not called us unto uncleanness, but unto holiness."

i) Titus 2:14—Jesus Christ "gave himself for us that he might redeem us from all iniquity, and purify unto himself a people of his own, zealous of good works."

j) James 1:27—"Pure religion and undefiled before God and the Father is this: to visit the fatherless and widows in their affliction, and to keep oneself unspotted from the world."

k) 1 Peter 1:15—"As he who hath called you is holy, so be ye holy in all manner of life."

1) 2 Peter 3:11—The lives of Christians should be characterized by "holy living and godliness."

m) 1 John 3:7—"Little children, let no man deceive you: he that doeth righteousness is righteous."

n) 3 John 11—"Beloved, follow not that which is evil, but that which is good."

There is a great deal of evidence that God wants us to be holy. Because the world endeavors to incite us to be evil, John says we cannot love that system and still say we love God. Philo, the first century Jewish philosopher, said it is as impossible for the love of the world to coexist with the love of God as it is impossible for light and darkness to coexist (quoted by John of Damascus [*Parall. Sacra* A, Tit. xxx. p. 370]). The distinguishing mark of a Christian is that he does not want to sin. Rather, he desires to be holy. When he does sin, he cries out with repentance as did David, "Create in me a clean heart, O God, and renew a right spirit within me" (Ps. 51:10).

2. The defilement of the world

First John 2:15 says that we should not only not love the system in general, but also the things that are in it. You might not love the system, but you might be attracted to the things that are in it. What are some examples? This world has godless religion, materialistic economics, and self-centered morality. We are not to be enamored of those things because they are inconsistent with who we are and how we are to live.

Some people say, "It's so hard to live a pure life today." It's always been hard, but the media today has probably made it more difficult to maintain a pure life. There's no sense in watching a movie that is filled with profanity, violence, and sexual immorality. Exposing yourself to things like that is only going to allow your mind to be preoccupied with the world's value system. Have you ever carefully listened to the music of the world? I like many kinds of music, but the ideas that are conveyed through the music of the world rarely square with what the Word of God says. If your ears are constantly bombarded by such music, you may find yourself following the world's morality. The same is true with television: When you watch it, you are sold the world's standards in a very slick way. The system is geared to generate sin, and if you want to play with it, it will generate sin in your life. If you want to put yourself in the world's mold—its materialism, humanism, and immorality—you are going against the very nature of your identity in Christ. Since we are called to "shine as lights in the world" (Phil. 2:15), we had better make sure people can see that there's something different about us. We need to disconnect ourselves from the system by saturating our minds with the Word of God to establish the right thought patterns.

B. The Content of the World (v. 16)

"For all that is in the world, the lust of the flesh, the lust of the eyes, and the pride of life, is not of the Father, but is of the world."

1. The lust of the flesh

   a) Defined

   This is the first of three areas in which Satan incites people to sin through his worldly system. Normally it brings to mind sexual immorality, but this kind of "lust" is much broader than that. The word in the Greek text is *epithumia*. It generally has an evil connotation, referring to a strong desire for satisfaction that is evil. The "flesh" is the part of man that is prone to sin, which man acquired when Adam rebelled against God. It is the rebellious self in us that wants to sin.

To identify it further, let me take you to Romans 7, where Paul gives insight into this particular part of man. Verses 15-17 say, "That which I do I understand not; for what I would [do], that do I not; but what I hate, that do I. If, then, I do that which I would not, I consent unto the law that it is good. Now, then, it is no more I that do it, but sin that dwelleth in me." Paul describes the fleshly human nature, saying, "There's something in me that wants to do good, but I just can't seem to do it. At the same time, even though something in me says, 'Don't do that,' I end up doing it anyway." There is a propensity for evil in human nature, even among Christians. For that reason, Paul could say, "I know that in me (that is, in my flesh) dwelleth no good thing" (v. 18). The flesh in its spiritual sense has nothing good about it. It is our evil propensity to sin.

b) Delineated

The flesh produces all kinds of terrible things. Galatians 5 gives a list of manifestations of the lust of the flesh that can loosely be categorized into four areas:

(1) Immorality

Verse 19 says, "The works of the flesh are manifest, which are these: adultery, fornication, uncleanness, lasciviousness." Although "adultery" doesn't appear in the best Greek manuscripts, "fornication" would include any type of sex outside of marriage, including homosexuality and bestiality. Besides sexual sin, the flesh also produces "uncleanness," which refers to impurity in thought and action, and "lasciviousness," which means "sensuality." A person characterized by the latter would be living only to please his pleasure-sensitive appetites.

(2) Idolatry

The flesh not only touches the sexual area but also includes the religious. Verse 20 mentions "idolatry" and "sorcery" (Gk., *pharmakia*). The latter is related to occultic practices and drugs, which have always been a part of pagan idolatry.

(3) Interpersonal relationships

The flesh tends to destroy our relationships with others. Verses 20-21 mention "hatred, strife, jealousy, wrath, factions, seditions, heresies, envyings, [and] murders."

(4) Indulgence

Man can't even control himself when it comes to alcohol. If the flesh is not restrained, its desires can result in "drunkenness, revelings [wild parties], and the like" (v. 21).

Verse 21 says that those who habitually indulge in the works of the flesh "shall not inherit the kingdom of God." Paul is saying that if you continue to do those kind of things, you could not possibly be a Christian. It is impossible for a Christian to regularly practice those things, because he is a child of God. Furthermore, he is indwelt by the Spirit, who gives him victory over the flesh. The Christian will hate sin. When you were saved, you became a partaker of the divine nature, which imparts the desire to do what pleases God. The world attacks us at the point of our weakness—the flesh. Satan seeks to influence us for his purposes through sexual abuse, false religion, strained relationships, and destructive indulgence. He uses his system to incite our flesh.

2. The lust of the eyes

Satan also incites us to sin through our eyes. Did you know that your eyes can get you into a lot of trouble? Perhaps blind people have an advantage in living a righteous life. The Bible gives us some illustrations about people who faced this area of lust.

a) Joshua 7:1-26—Achan saw some of the spoils of Jericho as the Israelites were conquering it. He took some things and buried them under his tent, even though the Lord had commanded Israel not to take anything from the city for themselves. Achan's disobedience cost him his life.

b) 2 Samuel 11:1-17—David was up on his roof, which was higher than everyone else's since he was king. While there, he saw Bathsheba bathing. If he had been a blind man, the act of adultery that followed would have never happened. The consequences of that sin were an illegitimate child, the murder of Bathsheba's husband, and the eventual destruction of David's family. Even one of his own sons tried to kill him.

c) Matthew 5:27-29—Jesus talked about the lust of the eyes when He said, "Ye have heard that it was said by them of old, Thou shalt not commit adultery; but I say to you that whosoever looketh on a woman to lust after her hath committed adultery with her already in his heart. And if thy right eye offend thee, pluck it out, and cast it from thee; for it is profitable for thee that one of thy members should perish, and not that thy whole body should be cast into hell." If you have a problem with the lust of the eyes, you may have to take some drastic measures to change what you're looking at. If you want to sit there and stare at immorality on TV, at the movies, or in magazines, you are opening yourself up to becoming programmed to lust.

d) Job 31:1—Women in Job's day wore robes. (I don't know what possibly could have excited men about a woman then unless it was her wrist.) However, Job gave us a wise principle for avoiding the lust of the eyes. He said, "I have made a covenant with my eyes; how then could I gaze at a virgin?" (NASB). Job was a smart man. He knew you're not going to get in trouble if you keep your eyes looking at the right things.

In our culture, we see things and want to buy them. It's almost impossible to keep on driving the same car. It's so easy to think of forty-nine reasons for getting rid of it. Clothes are more than simple covering. Today stores pressure us to be stylish and improve our image. We are bewitched by beauty. We drive in a different neighborhood and then become dissatisfied with the houses we live in. We need to have the attitude of the psalmist who says in Psalm 119:37, "Turn away my eyes from looking at vanity" (NASB). Satan wants us to desire things that are beyond what God wants us to have. Our eyes have an appetite. You've probably heard people say,

"Feast your eyes on that beauty!" Knowing that our eyes can lead us to lust, Satan uses his system to allure us into satisfying our appetites.

3. The pride of life

The third bridge to sin is "the pride of life." The Greek word *alazoneia* refers to being proud when you really have nothing to be proud about. For example, a pauper shows his friends when they come to town a fleet of ships that he claims to own, when in reality none of them belong to him. He would be bragging about something he doesn't have. It's one thing to have something great and brag about it; it's something else to have nothing and brag about it. The pride of life puts on a big show for other people. A person might be able to get by with a certain item, but he may want to get a better item to impress people with. People often live beyond what they can afford because they want others to think they have more than they have. Such a motive is boastful.

The apostle John identifies the three springs of evil in a climaxing sequence: sensuality, covetousness, and pride. Sensuality is the corruption of the lower part of man's nature— his base desires. Covetousness is the corruption of a higher part. It is a selfish desire for what is beautiful, whether it is a woman, a car, a house, or a dress. But pride is the highest corruption of man's being. It is the exaltation of man himself. By sensuality man sinks to the level of animals; by covetousness he competes on the level of men; by pride he tries to reach to the heights of God. The world is set to draw you into sin. Christians cannot love the world because of what it is—the enemy; who we are—the family of God; what it does—causes iniquity; and where it is going—to its end.

IV. BECAUSE OF WHERE THE WORLD IS GOING (v. 17)

A. Its Passing Discussed

Verse 17 presents a stark contrast: "And the world passeth away, and the lust of it; but he that doeth the will of God abideth forever." It is the Christian who does the will of God. What is God's will? First Timothy 2:3-4 tells us that "God, our Savior . . . will have all men to be saved, and to come unto the knowledge of the truth." God's will is that people be saved. Those who are saved will abide forever, but the world and its followers will pass away. We can't love the world because of its destiny. We are eternal, and it is passing. The

59

two principles of life and death can't operate together. The church is an eternally living people; the world is a dead system.

The words "passeth away" (Gk., *paragetai*) are in the present tense and imply that the world is continuing to disintegrate. It is in the process of dissolution. We often wonder now how much longer our civilization can last. The world is going to self-destruct because sin produces death. The world is a dying system. Its institutions are crumbling little by little—the family, the judicial system, the government. Everything is breaking down because the world is plagued by sin, which operates on a death principle.

B. Its Passing Depicted

   1. The process of deterioration

      a) 2 Thessalonians 2:7—"The mystery of iniquity doth already work." Evil is getting worse to a degree that man never knew before.

      b) 2 Timothy 3:13—"Evil men and seducers shall become worse and worse."

The world is in the process of destroying itself. Believers are citizens of an eternal kingdom (Phil. 3:20). Therefore we should not attach ourselves to the world's decaying system. Christians do not love the world, which is passing away. We belong to a different dimension. We live in "heavenly places" (Eph. 2:6).

   2. The peak of destruction

      a) The setting of the scene

         The final phases of self-destruction will come during the Tribulation, as seen in Revelation 6-19. The scene in chapter 5 depicts God sitting on His throne holding in His right hand a scroll, which is the title deed to the earth. (In effect, Satan took control of that title deed in the Garden of Eden.) An angel asks, "Who is worthy to open the scroll, and loose its seals?" (v. 2). Verses 6-7 say, "A Lamb as though it had been slain [Christ] . . . came and took the scroll out of the right hand of him that sat upon the throne."

         A Roman will was sealed so it could not be officially opened until after the death of the one who made it. This scroll that Christ took willed the earth to Him as its rightful heir. Beginning in chapter 6, our Lord breaks the seals, and terrible things start to happen.

b) The retribution upon the rejectors

(1) The seals

First comes the Antichrist on a white horse, pretending to be the Christ (v. 2). Peace is taken from the earth, and men start to kill each other (v. 4). All of a sudden sin reaches a climax, and everything in the dying system falls apart. A terrible famine strikes, as indicated by the phrase "a measure of wheat for a denarius" (v. 6). In other words, one meal's worth of wheat would cost a day's wages. The oil and the wine were to be left untouched for the rich people (v. 6). Death rampages the world, and one-fourth of the earth's inhabitants are killed "with sword, and with hunger, and with death, and with the beasts of the earth" (v. 8).

During this three-and-a-half-year period of worldwide catastrophe there will be "a great earthquake, and the sun [will become] as black as sackcloth of hair, and the moon [will become] like blood; and the stars of heaven [will fall] unto the earth, even as a fig tree casteth her untimely figs, when she is shaken of a mighty wind. And the heaven [will depart] as a scroll when it is rolled together; and every mountain and island [will be] moved out of their places" (vv. 12-14).

(2) The trumpets

The prophetic description of the judgment of these last times continues in chapter 8: After the first trumpet of judgment sounds, "there followed hail and fire mixed with blood, and they were cast upon the earth; and the third part of the trees was burnt up, and all green grass was burnt up" (v. 7). When the second angel sounds his trumpet, "a great mountain burning with fire was cast into the sea; and the third part of the sea became blood; and the third part of the creatures which were in the sea, and had life, died; and the third part of the ships were destroyed" (vv. 8-9). This chain of reactions is perhaps initiated by some kind of a meteorite. Then comes a terrible contamination of fresh water: "The third part of the waters became wormwood; and many men died of the waters, because they were made bitter" (v. 11).

As the fourth angel sounds his trumpet, God judges time: "The third part of the sun was smitten, and the third part of the moon, and the third part of the stars, so that the third part of them was darkened, and the day shown not for a third part of it, and the night likewise" (v. 12). The whole universe starts to fall apart. But that is only the beginning. The next trumpets announce events even worse. With the sixth trumpet, a third part of civilization is killed by fire, smoke, and brimstone (9:18). People continue to worship demons and refuse to repent of their acts of murder, sorcery, fornication, and robbery (vv. 20-21).

c) The end of the economy

Then in chapter 18, the entire evil system that Satan built is wiped out. Revelation 18:9 says, "The kings of the earth, who have committed fornication and lived luxuriously with her [the system] shall bewail her, and lament for her, when they shall see the smoke of her burning." When the system is gone, including its culture, economics, religion, and government, the unbelievers who are still alive will cry in despair. When judgment comes, "the merchants of the earth shall weep and mourn over her; for no man buyeth their merchandise any more: the merchandise of gold, and silver, and precious stones, and pearls, and fine linen, and purple, and silk, and scarlet, and all thyine wood, and all kinds of vessels of ivory, and all kinds of vessels of most precious wood, and of bronze, and iron, and marble, and cinnamon, and incense, and ointments, and frankincense, and wine, and oil, and fine flour, and wheat, and cattle, and sheep, and horses, and chariots, and slaves, and souls of men. And the fruits that thy soul lusted after are departed from thee . . . and thou shalt find them no more at all. The merchants of [the world] . . . shall stand afar off for the fear of her torment, weeping and wailing, and saying, Alas, alas, that great city" (vv. 11-16).

Even the music of the world will cease: "And the voice of harpers, and minstrels, and flute players, and trumpeters shall be heard no more at all in thee; and no craftsmen, of whatever craft he be, shall be found any more in thee; and the sound of a millstone shall be heard no more at all in thee" (v. 22).

d) The voices of victory

As the world's system is being destroyed, there will be voices in heaven saying, "The kingdom of this world is become the kingdom of our Lord, and of his Christ, and he shall reign forever and ever" (Rev. 11:15).

Christians do not love the world because of where it is going. First Corinthians 7:31 says, "The fashion of this world passeth away." Let's not even flirt with it. We shouldn't love it because it is our enemy, because we are part of God's family, because it incites us to sin, and because we have a different destiny.

If you're a Christian, you have overcome the world. So act like it! If you're not a Christian, you are a part of a system that is self-destructing. You're being victimized by Satan, the god of this world—and you probably thought you were doing what you wanted. That's tragic. Please understand that Jesus Christ can change your life when you put your faith in Him and accept what He's done for you. He will take you out of the world's evil system and give you eternal life. That's His promise.

Focusing on the Facts

1. Explain how man sold his birthright to the world (see p. 50).
2. Although the system that dominates the world is in the control of Satan, what did Jesus know He would do someday (see p. 50)?
3. How did Satan first counteract the truth in Genesis 4? What indication is there that Cain was basing his acceptance before God on his own effort (see p. 51)?
4. What do all false religions claim about how man enters God's presence (see p. 51)?
5. Satan used things like crime, arguments, riots, and wars to destroy what (see p. 51)?
6. Is Satan directly responsible for everything that the world does? Explain (see p. 52).
7. What does the world's system incite us to do (see p. 53)?

8. What do Christians serve, after having been servants of sin (Rom. 6:17-18; see p. 53)?
9. What has made it difficult to maintain a pure life in our modern society (see p. 55)?
10. What do the words *lust* and *flesh* mean in the context of 1 John 2:16 (see pp. 55-56)?
11. What are some ways the flesh manifests itself (Gal. 5:19-21; see pp. 56-57)?
12. What will those who habitually indulge in the works of the flesh never inherit, according to Galatians 5:21 (see p. 57)?
13. Explain how the lust of the eyes got Achan and David into trouble (see pp. 57-58).
14. Describe the person who is characterized by "the pride of life" (v. 16; see p. 59).
15. Differentiate between the corruptions of sensuality, covetousness, and pride (see p. 59).
16. Why is the world in the process of breaking down (see p. 60)?
17. When will the final phases of the world's destruction come (see p. 60)?
18. When the Lord breaks the seals on the scroll in Revelation 6, what starts to take place (see p. 61)?
19. As the world's system is being completely destroyed, what will be the response from heaven (Rev. 11:15; see p. 63)?

Pondering the Principles

1. If you are a Christian, are you living the holy life that the Lord expects of you? According to Titus 2:14, why did Jesus Christ sacrifice Himself for us? What does that verse say our heartfelt response ought to be to that purposeful act of love? As you meditate on Titus 2:11-14, evaluate how well your life-style is fitting into God's purposes.

2. Knowing that we are conditioned to accept the world's values through secular media, we must carefully evaluate the kinds of things that we expose our eyes and ears to. Is TV programming you with its distorted perspective of human relationships and materialism? Its influence on you may have been so gradual and subtle that it has been hardly noticeable. Have you become so worldly that it is difficult to tell you apart from an unbeliever who attends church? Based on your understanding of the Word of God, examine yourself to see how brightly your life shines in the world as a lighthouse of truth to the people lost on the sea of secularism.

3. Do you find yourself concentrating on satisfying your pleasure-sensitive appetites, which can only be temporarily appeased? Or are you consistently "trying to learn what is pleasing to the Lord" (Eph. 5:10, NASB) with whom you will spend eternity? Commit yourself to saturating your mind with the Word of God and to letting the Spirit lead you in accordance with the Scripture He inspired.

4. The lust of the eyes is a major problem in our sex-oriented and materialistic society. If you are a male who struggles with the sin of lusting for someone other than your spouse, make a covenant with your eyes, like Job did in Job 31:1. Recognize that an illicit relationship dishonors God and hinders the development of a healthy relationship based on honesty and trust. As you communicate with members of the opposite sex, concentrate on looking only into their eyes. If material possessions cause you to lust, meditate on Matthew 6:19-33 to refocus your perspective.

5. Praise God that you are part of an eternal kingdom that He has graciously allowed you to enter. Thank Him that you will be preserved from the terrible time of the Tribulation that will come upon those who have rejected Christ. Meditate on 2 Thessalonians 2:8-17.

Scripture Index